UNIVERSAL
PROCESS MODELING
PROCEDURE:
The Practical Guide to High-Quality
Business Process Models Using BPMN

Edmund A. Metera

Universal Process Modeling Procedure:

The Practical Guide to High-Quality Business Process Models Using BPMN

Copyright © 2018, 2022 by Edmund A. Metera

ISBN 978-1-7249149-8-9

Published by:

www.ProcessModelingAdvisor.com

and

Kindle Direct Publishing

Disclaimer

This book was written as a practical guide for business process modeling. The statements made and opinions expressed are the personal observations and assessments of the author based on his own experiences, and are not intended to prejudice any party. There may be errors or omissions in this guide. The author or publisher does not accept any liability or responsibility for any loss or damage caused or alleged to have been caused by the use of the information in this manual. Errors or omissions will be corrected in future editions, provided the publisher receives written notification.

DEDICATION

For my wife Shell, and daughter Victoria.

CONTENTS

PREFACE

Despite proven process management and information technology (IT) methodologies, excellent modeling tools, robust modeling notations (like Business Process Modeling and Notation), and all the well-intentioned efforts of business analysts and modeling participants, there still are a lot of ineffective business process models out there. Why? More than anything else, a business process model's quality relies upon the competence of the business or process analyst. That competence is marked by an effective, consistently practiced approach for producing a business process model in the face of unique project dynamics, like resource constraints, opportunities, methodologies, available tools and notations, time constraints, and stakeholders who each have unique experiences and perspectives.

And times have changed. Strictly procedural notions and notations were invented in the days of procedural language programming. Today, a high-quality business process structure has been conceived, structured, and can be readily configured as a collaborating network of event-driven, outcome-oriented services, not just as a sequential procedure.

This book gives you a defined, proven method for producing a high-quality business process model within any project: The Universal Process Modeling Procedure (UPMP). It demonstrates how to meet the unique requirements, opportunities, and constraints of any process modeling engagement. It gives you concise agendas for eliciting the model's content. It shows you how to elicit, perceive, normalize and unequivocally define processes and activities at any scale and degree of abstraction. It shows you how to illustrate process model scope and process flow, and the most common types of business process flow diagram refinements using BPMN. It also shows you how to determine if your model is of high enough quality.

INTRODUCTION

This book is a guide for producing high-quality business process models.

Business process models may be called for in various business process management (BPM) and information technology (IT) methodologies.

- Business process improvement frameworks such as Total Quality Management and methodologies like Six Sigma use process maps or flowcharts.

- According to the International Institute of Business Analysis (IIBA), scope modeling, process modeling, and elicitation techniques (e.g., interviews, observations, etc.) are techniques performed by a business analyst.

- According to the American Society for Quality (ASQ), a process flowchart is a primary tool for process analysis, prescribed for understanding a work process.

- Many application software implementation methodologies employ business process models as functional/workflow specifications, test cases, training materials, or operations documentation for application software.

Project methodology, rigor, modeling tools, project scope, and key project stakeholders vary widely, and these dynamics are typically beyond a business analyst's control. What a business analyst can control and bring to the table is his or her competence in producing a model that meets that project's unique needs, opportunities, and constraints. That competence is demonstrated by the use of a consistent approach that is tailored to each project's methodology, tools, and stakeholders' expectations.

In this Practical Guide To High-Quality Business Process Models, you will learn about:

- The six-step Universal Process Modeling Procedure (UPMP) for producing high-quality business process models.

- The four-part Universal Business Process Definition and the business process normalization technique, that you can use to perceive, normalize and unequivocally define any candidate business process or activity.

- The business process model components that are produced at each step and how they are related. The productivity and quality benefits that come with the defined process (UPMP) that incorporates quality assurance and control, best-suited notation and tools, clear elicitation agendas, and elicitation techniques.

- The Universal elicitation agendas that focus elicitation effort on the right business process model content.

- The model components that can comprise each business process model and whose configuration can be tailored to suit the unique mission, constraints, and opportunities of each project.

- The quality of business process models can be consistently measured according to Universal Business Process Model Quality Factors.

What This Book Is About

This book is about <u>HOW</u> to produce high-quality business process models.

This book is about how to develop a high-quality business process model for any project following a defined, proven, step-by-step method called the Universal Process Modeling Procedure (UPMP); how to perceive, normalize and unequivocally define modern, sound process and activity structures; and to use Business Process Modeling and Notation (BPMN) to illustrate scope diagrams and business process flow diagrams.

The Landscape chapter covers topics that influence how business process modeling is performed. It provides practical answers to the following common process modeling questions:

- What are business process model uses?
- What is Business Process Modeling and Notation?
- What are elicitation techniques?
- What are business process model quality approaches?
- What real-world variables influence each model?
- What is process-modeling competence?

The Introduction to UPMP chapter introduces the process modeling approach that is detailed throughout the rest of this book. It answers these questions about business process modeling:

- What is the Universal Process Modeling Procedure (UPMP)?
- What does the UPMP produce?
- What are the UPMP elicitation agendas?

The Business Process Normalization chapter introduces a modern business process paradigm. It shows you how to apply it to achieve sound, modern business process structures:

- What are the benefits of business process normalization?
- What is the Universal Business Process Definition?
- How to perceive all business processes and activities.
- How to normalize any business process or activity.

The next six chapters detail the six UPMP steps. Each describes how to effectively elicit, illustrate, produce, and validate one component of a high-quality business process model:

- How to elicit, define and document a business process model's mission.
- How to elicit and illustrate a business process model's scope.
- How to identify, define and document business activities.
- How to elicit and model basic business process flow.
- How to elicit and model business process flow refinements.

- How to elicit feedback about business process model quality.

Following the Conclusion, the Appendices offer consolidated elicitation agendas, quality checklist and BPMN event subtype examples.

It Is Not About …

This book is not about any specific business process improvement/management or IT methodology, software design techniques, process modeling software, nor is it a BPMN reference manual.

Project methodologies, technologies, software design techniques, elicitation techniques, modeling tools and the degree to which they are applied from one project to the next vary widely.

This book does not prescribe a specific business IT or business process improvement project methodology because the UPMP is effective with a full spectrum of BPM and IT methodologies.

This book is not about software design using BPMN. With the exception of workflow configuration models in no-code and low-code platforms, most business analysts and quality improvement analysts do not design software. The first step of the UPMP will be to clearly determine why a process model is needed and what it will be used for in a given project.

Process model content can be illustrated using any process modeling software, whiteboard, or even pencil and paper. Therefore, this book does not prescribe any specific modeling software.

Finally, this book interprets and demonstrates how to use BPMN to graphically communicate meaningful process information. It demonstrates how to follow BPMN syntactical rules well enough to meet the mission of almost any business process model. It is not intended to be the definitive source of BPMN notation, nor does it intend to demonstrate BPMN's use in software code generation.

How to Use This Book

This book is organized according to the Universal Process Modeling Procedure (UPMP).

This book is organized and written in a prescriptive, practical how-to fashion. Read through the whole book in chapter sequence to learn the Universal Process Modeling Procedure as a whole, and then return to the appropriate chapters while producing a process model, to review how to elicit and model or document each model component.

This book uses the terms "process" and "business process" interchangeably. And the term process includes its alias, workflow. The business process modeling procedure described here can be applied to produce conceptual, logical, and configuration models of manual and/or automated processes. Since BPMN's origins lie in software development, business process models that are documented using BPMN can elegantly describe logical software requirements, design, and configuration. However, very many if not most process models are developed and consumed in business process improvement or management methodologies. BPMN can communicate rich conceptual, logical, and configuration models of processes for those purposes too.

Use the Landscape chapter to orient or validate your education, experiences, expectations, and rationale for establishing or improving business process modeling competence.

Use the Introduction to UPMP chapter as a summary reference to the Universal Process Modeling Procedure's steps, expected outcomes, and products of each step.

The Universal Business Process Definition has its dedicated chapter so that you can easily come back and refer to its fundamental paradigm and the business process normalization technique, throughout your business process elicitation, perception, definition, and modeling journey.

The main body of this book is organized according to the steps of the UPMP. After reading each of these chapters, the reader should be able to answer four questions about each UPMP step:

- What is the purpose of this step?
- What business process model component should I produce in this step?
- What questions should I ask to elicit the content of this business process model component?
- How would I document or illustrate what I've elicited?

The conclusion summarizes how using the UPMP will establish or improve a business process modeling competence.

Finally, use the appendices as quick references for 1) consolidated Universal business process model elicitation agendas; and 2) consolidated Universal process model quality checklists.

BUSINESS PROCESS MODELING LANDSCAPE

Any business process model is shaped by its expected benefits and uses, notation, elicitation techniques, quality approach, real-world opportunities and constraints, and ultimately, the modeler's competence.

Projects are by definition, unique and temporary. They all have a unique mix of methodologies, tools, notations, elicitation techniques, quality expectations, opportunities, constraints, and the competency of the business analyst producing the model. All these factors influence a business process model's development, and ultimately its utility and quality.

A competent process modeler understands how to act on these business process modeling principles:

- Business process models are products that are produced and consumed in business process management or information technology projects.
- BPMN is well suited for illustrating business process scope and flow.
- Effective use of elicitation techniques is crucial for achieving a high-quality business process model.
- Quality assurance and quality control techniques also contribute to a high-quality business process model.
- Every project comes with unique opportunities and constraints.
- A business process model's quality is ultimately dependent on the competence of the modeler.

This book demonstrates how to use BPMN elements to illustrate conceptual and logical business process scope, process flow and process flow refinements that are good enough for a wide range of business process management or improvement and information technology methodologies.

Process Improvement or Management Uses

Business process models are produced and used in process improvement and management project methodologies.

Business process management (BPM) or improvement methodologies use process models (also known as process maps) to specify and measure business operations and to help identify and measure improvements. Some examples of BPM or improvement methodologies include Total Quality Management, Continuous Process Improvement, Six Sigma, and Lean Six Sigma. Business process models' uses within business process management or improvement methodologies can be:

Enterprise Management – Business process models are used by management to make decisions about current or future organization, staff, systems, budgets, etc. based on business function or process architecture as part of an enterprise architecture.

Regulatory or Standards Compliance – Business managers may prepare and use business process models to comply with operational regulations or standards. Just a few examples of process related regulations or standards are:

- Current Good Manufacturing Practice (cGMP) – Process standards relating to health business domains.
- International Standards Organization (ISO) – Process standards relating to 97 different business domains.
- Capability Maturity Model Integration (CMMI) – Process improvement standards relating to any business domain.
- Sarbanes Oxley Act (SOXA) – Regulations relating to accounting practices of publicly traded corporations.

Productivity and Quality Improvement – Functional managers, business analysts, quality analysts, and operational staff use business process models to define and baseline current business processes, and then propose, implement and measure operational improvements to those same business processes.

Process Integration or Outsourcing – Functional managers, quality managers, and operational staff may use business process models to integrate business processes of business units or companies.

Training – Functional managers, business analysts, and trainers may use business process models to transfer knowledge about the scope and sequence of business activities that are to be performed.

Information Technology Uses

Business process models are produced and used in information technology (IT) project methodologies.

Business process models' uses within IT projects can be:

Functional System Requirements – Business and systems analysts use business process models to specify the conceptual or logical functional requirements of an automated system.

Test Cases – Test managers and systems analysts may reuse logical business process models to outline or specify the steps of functional test cases.

System Architecture – Business and systems analysts use business process models to specify automated systems' conceptual or logical boundaries and the relationships among system services.

Software Logic – Systems analysts and software programmers may use business process models to specify the internal logic of a software component.

Examples of IT methodologies that prescribe business process models include:

- The International Institute of Business Analysis Body of Knowledge (IIBA BoK) is a framework for business analysis activities. It identifies scope modeling and process modeling as core competencies of a business analyst.

- The Open Group Architecture Framework is a framework and methodology for describing enterprise models. It includes process models among its architecture models.
- Any waterfall software development methodology can use a business process model throughout its functional requirements, design, construction, testing, and deployment phases.
- IT Infrastructure Library (ITIL) service management framework calls for business process models among its Strategy, Design, Transition, Operation, and Continual Service Improvement phases.
- Unified Process is a software development methodology. It calls for business process models in its Concept, Initiation, and Implementation phases.

Business Process Modeling and Notation (BPMN)

BPMN is well-suited for illustrating the scope and flow of today's business processes and enabling technologies, like the Internet.

A picture is worth a thousand words. In the same way that house plans use graphical objects that we can all recognize, process models also rely on a notation that illustrates important aspects of a process and that can be easily understood by the model's readers.

Examples of process modeling notations include flow charts, functional decomposition diagrams, data flow diagrams, and use case diagrams (part of UML). Some of these notations, like functional decomposition and data flow diagrams, have been around since the 1960s. Universal Markup Language has offered some business process modeling innovation since the 1990s. However, business organizations and technologies have profoundly moved forward since then. Distributed teams, remote work, the internet, and cloud computing services have changed the world. It is difficult, if not impossible to elicit and illustrate modern process elements using notations of the past.

Business Process Modeling and Notation (BPMN) was defined by the Business Process Modeling Initiative (BPMI) and is maintained by the Object Modeling Group (OMG). BPMI states that the goal of BPMN is:

"To provide a notation that is readily understandable by all business users."

BPMN is perhaps the best-suited notation for illustrating a modern business process structure. It includes explicit symbols for illustrating concepts that are relevant to today's systems and business processes, namely events and messaging.

Events and messaging are integral to the way many of today's business processes work, enabled by technologies like cloud computing. Cloud services can be implemented across different geographies, organizations, and/or systems and synchronized within a single business process. The same service or activity may be used within different business processes without controlling or being controlled by any of them. Cloud services don't just start and end. They are initiated in response to events, and they achieve expected outcomes.

BPMN's graphic icons for events and messages enhance the way a business analyst can perceive and model modern business processes. The Universal Business Process Definition in this book uses initiating events and expected outcomes, not just activity, to perceive and define a modern business process structure. BPMN also allows us to illustrate how a business process may be interrupted by events, and how a process may collaborate with other processes without controlling them, via messaging.

Since BPMN's roots are in software design and process automation, examples of uses and more exacting adherence to the BPMN notational standard in those contexts are the subject of other references.

The full BPMN standard is published by www.OMG.org. To learn more about the BPMN standard, refer to the Business Process Model and Notation (BPMN), Version 2.0.2, or later. URL: http://www.omg.org/spec/BPMN.

Elicitation Techniques

Elicitation techniques are performed to gather a business process model's content.

Elicitation is how a business analyst discovers the content of a business process model. The International Institute of Business Analysis defines elicitation in *A Guide to the Business Analysis Body of Knowledge*:

"An activity within requirements development that identifies sources for requirements and then uses elicitation techniques to gather requirements from those sources."

Common elicitation techniques include workshops, interviews, observations, documentation reviews (studies), and existing system reviews. Their practical advantages and disadvantages are briefly described below:

Workshop - A workshop is a good way to build consensus when there are diverse key stakeholders in the business process. It's also a good form of teambuilding. However, if workshop participants are not suitably knowledgeable, willing, or available, then the process modeling will not be successful. Another potential pitfall is that if the workshop's facilitator (i.e., business analyst) lacks effective workshop facilitation skills, the process modeling will not be successful.

Interview - Interviews with individual key stakeholders are generally easier to arrange and facilitate than a workshop with a group. However, more follow-up effort and time may be ultimately be needed to reconcile viewpoints that differ among individual key stakeholders.

Documentation Reviews - Reviewing documentation is a great way of reusing previously completed work. However, existing documentation may be prone to have errors and omissions for the model's scope or required degree of abstraction. What was documented in the past may no longer accurately or completely describe current operations or requirements. Another pitfall of documentation review is that it may not reflect or include current key stakeholders' knowledge or expectations.

Observation – The advantage of observations is that they are indisputable, or at least leave little room for speculation. They are a great way to corroborate what has been initially elicited by documentation reviews, interviews or workshops. A shortfall of observations is that only a subset of activities may be physically observable. For example, you can observe a user's interactions with a software system, but not the software's internal logic.

Existing System Review - Existing system reviews can be performed independently and with less total effort than workshops and interviews. However, not all automated activities are observable or documented. Elicitation of automated activities and logic relies upon software configuration or programming knowledge.

How to Choose Elicitation Techniques

Select elicitation technique(s) based on the unique opportunities and constraints of each project.

Selecting the best-suited elicitation techniques is one of the keys to producing the right content and a high-quality model. To make the most effective use of elicitation and modeling effort, a business analyst should choose elicitation techniques by consciously asking and answering:

"What elicitation techniques are best-suited to the modeling mission and unique opportunities and constraints of this project?"

Considering factors such as the mission of the model, project opportunities and constraints, what modeling has already been completed, and the model component or type of refinement currently being elicited, the answer may be a mix of elicitation techniques. For example, a business analyst may choose to review existing documentation before conducting a workshop, then supplement what is learned in the workshop with follow-up interviews and observations, and then return to documentation. A face-to-face meeting or workshop can also be a good way to validate completed business process model content with a project's key stakeholders.

Quality Assurance and Control

Quality assurance and quality control are two approaches to achieving a high-quality product.

A business process model is a product in a BPM or IT project and its quality influences a BPM or IT project's overall outcome. If the process model's quality is high, then its influence will be good decision-making, reduced rework costs, and improved chances of achieving desired project outcomes. Everyone expects a high-quality model. The challenge is how to deliver that.

Two approaches that can be used to achieve a high-quality business process model are quality assurance and quality control. A quality assurance approach involves establishing and consistently following a defined procedure for a product, measuring the results, and continuously improving on them. Quality control entails ensuring that a product meets quality expectations before it is deemed complete.

The Universal Business Process Modeling Procedure Quality employs both quality assurance and quality control approaches to achieve high-quality business process models.

First, the UPMP is a defined process for producing business process models. A business analyst who adopts the already-defined and well-proven UPMP as his or her process modeling approach will start with a defined level of competence. They can repeat, measure and improve their competence from there, with practice, from one project to the next.

Second, the UPMP includes a quality control step. The purpose of Step 6 – Validate the Business Process Model – is to validate that the quality criteria for a business process model are sufficiently present.

Real-World Opportunities and Constraints

Unique opportunities and constraints come with every project.

According to the Project Management Institute's Body of Knowledge, **every project is a unique, temporary endeavor**.

In the real world of a business analyst, each project comes with unique opportunities and constraints that influence a process model's development. Some types of real-world opportunities and constraints include:

- The number, business experience, and availability of people to participate in elicitation activities, such as workshops and/or interviews;
- The business analyst's business domain knowledge and experience;
- The business analyst's elicitation and modeling skills;
- The organizational assets, including methodologies, tools, standards, and previous work, that are available to the project;
- Elicitation techniques (observation, interviews, etc.) that can feasibly be performed on that project ;
- Omissions made in previous efforts and discoveries that are yet to be made by the project; and
- The schedule and budget limits of the project. Two ubiquitous project constraints are time and money. Available resources need to be spent efficiently and effectively.

Because every project presents its unique opportunities and constraints, a competent business analyst will be prepared to tailor the steps, effort, elicitation and modeling activities, notations, tools used, as well as the configuration of each model from one project to the next.

Competence

Business process modeling competence is demonstrated by a consistent approach in the face of unique project opportunities and constraints.

There are many examples of poor-quality business process models out there. Many are of poor contextual quality. They don't accurately enough reflect what's going on in the business, or at least not in the views of key stakeholders. Many are of poor syntactical quality. They do not contain the types of information their readers want to see or do not follow the chosen notation well enough to communicate what is intended. A poor-quality business process model negatively affects the cost, timeliness, quality of decision-making, and the outcomes of the project of which it is a part.

Why are many business process models of poor contextual and/or syntactical quality?

- The methodologies and frameworks that prescribe the use of business process models typically don't prescribe how to produce business process models.

- The use of modeling notations varies. Even the use of standard notations like BPMN can vary widely from one business analyst to the next.

- Plenty of capable business process modeling tools are readily available, so model quality is not a technological problem. Process modeling tools do not themselves produce good models any more than carpentry tools without a skilled carpenter would produce good furniture.

- The projects that produce and consume business process models are by definition unique and temporary endeavors that come with their own real-world opportunities and constraints.

- Any business process model is influenced by the unique experience and motives of the modeler and the key stakeholders participating in the model's development. While motives may be similar, perceptions are certainly unique and often diverse.

- Sometimes process modeling is a very short process involving only one stakeholder – the business analyst. Other times, it's a long journey of discovery and validation involving many stakeholders across departments or enterprises.

- Competence varies widely among business analysts. Most rely on an ad-hoc, trial and error approach, having no formal training in process modeling, and produce models very infrequently.

While all these factors do vary from one project and business analyst to the next, the quality of business process models need not.

Business process model quality is ultimately dependent upon the competence of the business analyst doing the elicitation and documentation. That competence is demonstrated by a consistent, comprehensive, tailorable, and efficient approach from one project to the next, and tailored despite the methodologies, key stakeholders, notations, tools, and opportunities at play. Establishing or improving that competence is this book's focus.

By adopting and consistently following the defined and proven best practice, a business analyst will establish and can begin to continuously improve their process modeling productivity and quality. The six-step Universal Process Modeling Procedure (UPMP) is a defined and proven best practice. The UPMP approach is predictable and can be improved with practice. The UPMP approach can be tailored but still be followed despite the methodologies, key stakeholders, notations, tools, opportunities, and constraints that will always vary from one project to the next.

UNIVERSAL PROCESS MODELING PROCEDURE (UPMP)

Use the six-step UPMP to produce high-quality business process models.

The Universal Process Modeling Procedure (UPMP) is a defined and proven procedure. It can be applied within any BPM or IT project whose methodology requires a business process model. It includes six activities to be completed by a business analyst or whoever is responsible for producing the model. The expected outcome of the UPMP is a business process model that meets the needs of its BPM or IT project.

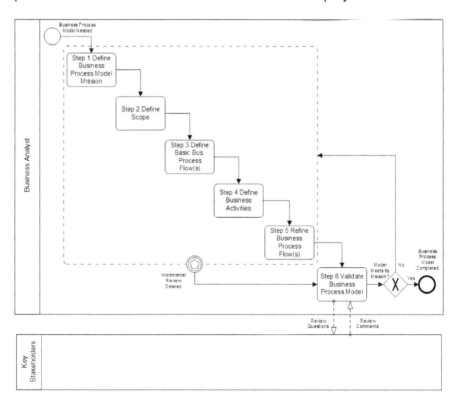

UPMP Step 1 – Define Business Process Model Mission

UPMP Step 1 is initiated by a BPM or IT project whose methodology requires a business process model. This step is comprised of eliciting and documenting the expected tense, required degree of abstraction, and intended use of the business process model. The expected outcome of UPMP Step 1 is a defined mission for the business process model. A clear mission statement will guide modeling decisions made by the business analyst and stakeholders who participate throughout the rest of the model's development.

UPMP Step 2 – Define Scope

UPMP Step 2 starts once the model's mission has been established, or when new project scope is discovered, causing the model's scope to be refined. The expected outcome of UPMP Step 2 is a defined functional boundary. External actors and the exchanges (aka "gives" and "gets") between a process or collection of processes and the surrounding actors define a boundary or scope. The scope diagram produced in this step will be used to focus the forthcoming process analysis activities.

UPMP Step 3 – Define Basic Business Process Flow(s)

UPMP Step 3 starts after the model's mission and the functional scope have been established. The expected outcome of UPMP Step 3 is to define how the business process may be initiated and the sequence (aka flow) of activities that lead to one or more of the expected outcomes. This step produces one or more basic process flow diagrams that will provide the foundation for Step 4 – Define Business Process Activities and Step 5 - Refine Business Process Flow(s).

UPMP Step 4 – Define Business Activities

Once UPMP Step 3 has established the basic business process flow, the task of defining the business activities in UPMP Step 4 can begin. The expected outcome of UPMP Step 4 is to define the business activities that comprise the business process. This step produces an Activity Catalogue that will be used and may be updated by Step 5 – Refine Business Process Flow(s), whenever business activities are discovered, redefined, or eliminated.

UPMP Step 5 – Refine Business Process Flow(s)

UPMP Step 5 starts once the basic business process flow and activity definitions have been established, or when review comments require further refinements or enhancements to the existing business process flow(s). The expected outcome of UPMP Step 5 is to elicit and document details about the business process flow(s) to the extent needed to meet this process model's unique mission. This step produces one or more refined and completed process flow diagrams.

UPMP Step 6 – Validate Business Process Model

UPMP Step 6 is started after the refined business process flow(s) have been completed. It may also be performed incrementally when any of the other UPMP steps are completed. The expected outcome of UPMP Step 6 is either that the model is agreed to meet its mission or that refinements to the model have been identified. This step produces either a high-quality business process model that will be consumed by the rest of a process improvement or IT project, or it produces review comments that will be used to implement further model refinements.

UPMP Products

The UPMP produces six key business process model components.

The UPMP creates the products that are typically found in a high-quality business process model. The products of each of the UPMP steps are illustrated and described below:

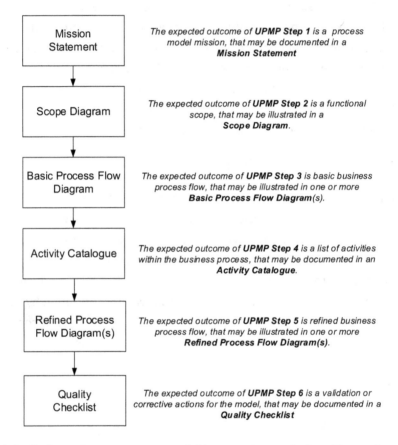

Model Mission – Every process model has a unique mission. That unique mission guides the development of remaining model content and composition. UPMP Step 1's product is a clear mission for the model. It specifies the expected tense, required degree of abstraction, and intended use of the model. The model's mission is embodied in a written or at least verbalized mission statement.

Scope Diagram – Every business process model has a boundary, which is known as its scope. UPMP Step 2's product is a clear identification of a boundary demarcated by exchanges with external actors, such as other organizations, processes, or roles. The process model's named boundary, as well as the exchanges with external actors, are graphically illustrated, in a scope diagram. (In some methodologies, a scope diagram is known as a "context diagram".)

Basic Business Process Flow Diagram(s) – The events that cause a process to begin, one or more activities, and the process' expected outcome(s) are typically achieved in a planned sequence, or "flow". This is its basic business process flow. A process model may contain one or more basic process flow diagrams. UPMP Step 3's product is one or more basic business process flow diagrams.

Activity Catalogue – Any process is comprised of one or more activities. UPMP Step 4's product is clear identification and definition of the business activities that comprise the process model. All in-scope activities and sub-activities are identified and defined in the model's Activity Catalogue. The Activity Catalogue contains the name and definition of each activity, and may also contain other "meta-data" (such as process measurement data). The Activity Catalogue is updated whenever new activities and sub-activities are discovered or defined.

Refined Process Flow Diagram(s) – A refined business process flow diagram is a result of refinements to a basic business process flow diagram. One process model may contain one or more refined business process flow diagrams to meet its mission. Types of process flow refinements include detailing or summarizing activities; specifying business decisions, exceptions, or assigned responsibilities; and more. UPMP Step 5's expected outcome is one or more process flow diagrams that have been refined to meet the model's unique mission.

Process Model Quality Checklist – Quality review checklists may also be included in the model's configuration. A high-quality process model is validated using specific contextual and syntactical quality criteria. UPMP Step 6's product is a completed quality checklist to validate whether or not the model meets certain quality criteria and therefore answer objectively whether the model is fit for its intended use or needs further refinement.

Each business process model's configuration should be tailored to suit that model's unique mission. For example, if the mission is to describe the scope of a project, then a business analyst should only produce a mission statement, scope diagram, and quality checklist. More often, the model's mission in a BPM or IT project will lead a business analyst to complete all UPMP steps and to produce a process model that is best comprised of all the UPMP products, including a mission statement, a scope diagram, one or more basic and refined process flow diagrams, an activity catalogue, and a quality checklist.

Universal Business Process Model Elicitation Agendas

Use clear, focused elicitation agendas to elicit business process model content.

Mark Twain is credited with essentially reminding us that "God gave us two ears and one mouth and we should use them accordingly." This is good advice while performing any type of elicitation. Yet, many business analysts still flounder, not because they fail to conduct elicitation techniques like workshops, interviews, and observations; not because they do not ask questions; not because they do not listen; and not because they are not genuinely seeking information. They flounder because they don't seek to answer the right questions. They lack a clear and concise elicitation agenda or set of questions that need to be answered by their elicitation activity. A competent business analyst has a clear agenda for elicitation that is focused on what is needed – in this case, business process model content.

Each UPMP step has a clear, concise elicitation agenda that is focused on eliciting the contextual information that comprises each component or refinement of the business process model.

These elicitation agendas are to be used along with any elicitation techniques that the business analyst may use. For example, the Universal basic business process flow elicitation agenda's questions are the same, whether they are answered via a workshop, documentation review, interview, etc. The forthcoming chapters describe how each UPMP step has its own concise Universal elicitation agenda.

These agendas are found together in Appendix 1 – Universal Business Process Model Elicitation Agendas.

Edmund A. Metera

BUSINESS PROCESS NORMALIZATION

Adopt and follow the four-part Universal Business Process Definition to elicit, perceive, define and normalize sound, modern business process structures.

For decades, business analysts, process analysts, and their stakeholders have tried to define business processes according to various characteristics:

- Processes transform inputs into outputs.
- Processes have internal or external customers.
- Processes can cross organizational boundaries.
- Processes can be defined from a stakeholder's viewpoint (enterprise or person).
- Processes can be conceptually, logically, or physically (configuration) described.
- Processes can be decomposed into lower-level processes and activities.
- Processes can "flow".
- Processes can cooperate with other processes.
- Processes are something that can be measured.
- According to the standard published by Object Management Group (www.omg.org), the organization responsible for standardizing modeling notations, including BPMN: *"A Process is any activity performed within a company or organization."*

While all of these statements are true and each may help us to perceive some dimension of a business process, none of them is complete enough to enable business analysts to elicit, perceive and unequivocally define sound, modern, business process structures. Some of these dimensions may just confuse the task at hand and make perceiving and defining business processes more difficult than it needs to be. If one were to elicit all these dimensions at the outset, one would consume substantial time and effort but may still not have a contextually clear definition of a process.

There will be about as many points of view and opinions about what any business process is as there are stakeholders in that process, at least at the start of the process analysis. As always, business analysts and process analysts need to be able to consistently perceive processes and facilitate the journey of business process elicitation, definition, and modeling, with their stakeholders. The pace and the technologies of modern, digital transformation, low-code, and no-code projects demand that business process and workflow elicitation, and definition be done in an efficient, competent way, instead of ad-hoc questioning and trial and error.

All of these challenges can be met. Any business process can be straightforwardly elicited, perceived, normalized, and unambiguously defined. Let's first consider housing. Any house, no matter its scale, degree of abstraction, location, building materials, and all its unique details, etc. must have a foundation, walls, and a roof to be a house. If it's missing any of those, it is not acceptable as a house. And for obvious productivity and quality reasons, those basic structural elements are established first, before it is practical to invest time and money in a home's other architectural, engineering or construction refinements.

The same is true for sound business process and workflow structures. Any business process must have a cohesive structure of basic elements to be considered a business process. Its basic structural elements should be elicited and consensus reached, before pursuing all of a process's possible details and refinements. Even after all desired process refinements have been applied, the process will still have its defining structural elements. This holds for any process or workflow structure, at any degree of abstraction (i.e. conceptual, logical, or configuration), a process' scale, or the unique details about a business process or workflow.

Business Process Normalization Benefits

Use Business Process Normalization to be more effective as a business analyst and to produce higher quality business process models.

Align with Modern Business Structures and Technologies. Processes that have been normalized according to the Universal Business Process Definition are event-driven and outcome-oriented. These structures can be readily implemented across enterprises' geographies and boundaries. They can be readily translated into modern networks of collaborating services (such as SaaS services in the cloud), just as well as traditional sequential procedures and workflow designs.

Be More Efficient. Whenever discovering and defining business processes among a group of stakeholders, it's more effective to be asking the right questions, than a lot of questions. The Universal Business Process Definition frames the elicitation and normalization agenda with four simple questions, whose answers can be doggedly pursued by the business analyst with the model's stakeholders.

Gain Contextual Quality. Assuming that everyone will understand the same meaning of the name of a business process is insufficient. By normalizing a business process according to the Universal Business Process Definition's four rules, the contextual knowledge and consensus about that process become unequivocal among readers of that definition.

Minimize Redundant Activities. An enterprise may have different processes that do the same thing but are named differently. Any two candidate business processes that, through process normalization, answer Business Process Normalization's four tests with the same answers are aliases of each other. There are very justifiably two different names for the same process. They should be re-examined to decide if one of them can be, feasibly eliminated.

Minimize Non-value-adding Activities. People, departments, and enterprises tend to propose or perform activities that they do, instead of what is needing to be done. Candidate activities that are not needed to achieve a process's outcome should be re-examined and either be discarded, or they may belong in another process.

Produce Well-Written Business Process Descriptions. The answers to the four business process normalization questions can be written in consistent and concise plain-language sentences to form contextually meaningful, unequivocal process descriptions.

Improve Reusable Service Potential. According to the Universal Business Process Definition, activities are themselves event-driven and outcome-oriented processes. Each is defined in-part and bounded by its initiating event and expected outcome. Event and outcome-oriented activities have the potential to be recognized as reusable services, reusable in more than one larger process.

Universal Business Process Definition

Adopt the four-part Universal Business Process Definition to elicit, perceive, and define sound, modern business process structures.

A business analyst just needs an unequivocal frame of reference for eliciting, perceiving, and defining any business process: the four-part Universal Business Process Definition.

Any business process is:

1. **a repeatable collection of interrelated work tasks,**

2. **initiated in response to a business event,**

3. **that achieves an expected business outcome,**

4. **for one or more customers of the process.**

These four common-sense rules define the basic but sound structure of all processes, workflows, and activities regardless of their scale, the model's degree of abstraction, the overarching project methodology, the modeling participants, and the organizations and the technologies that will implement them.

The resulting business process structures are high-quality structures because they have been elicited, perceived, and defined by asking and answering the right questions. They can be implemented equally well as traditional sequential procedures or as today's, distributed business structures and networked technical (like cloud services) architectures. As event-driven, outcome-oriented business process structures, they are also consistent with modern networked, collaborative business relationships and cloud technologies.

The practicality of this Universal Business Process Definition is demonstrated when training business analysts to use the UPMP.

The process modeling classes that I teach are typically comprised of business analysis students from different industries and backgrounds. Early in the class, students are asked to name examples of business processes from their own, familiar business domains. A random example is chosen and the student who provided it is asked to describe that process to the class. The initial response can vary from a single sentence to a minute-long monologue. The other students are then asked to pose questions that would clarify that business process's definition: What are the inputs? What are the outputs? How are the activities that comprise the process performed? Who performs the process? How often does the process occur? Many possible dimensions of that process can be discussed, and this questioning and answering can go on for five or ten minutes until the eyes of some of the students begin to glaze over. This exercise illustrates how the elicitation of a business process definition may be enthusiastic but unfocused.

When I ask the same student to describe the process again according to the four-part Universal Business Process Definition. He/she will identify for the rest of the class what causes the process to begin, mention one or more activities included in the process, the process' expected outcome, and who or what is the customer of the process, all within about 30 seconds and in just a few sentences. The description of the process, restated according to the Universal Business Process Definition, provides a more complete yet concise response. The other students invariably agree that they have a clear and more unified understanding, regardless of their differing initial perceptions and questions.

Already-competent business analysts and process analysts adopt and use the Universal Business Process Definition's four common-sense rules throughout their business process modeling journeys. They use it to guide their elicitation agendas with business stakeholders as they work out and arrive at high-quality, robust, predictable, and efficient business process structures.

Put On Your Business Process Sunglasses

Perceive all business processes at any scale or degree of abstraction using the four-part Universal Business Process Definition.

Many factors in the process modeling landscape can overwhelm a business analyst's perceptions. Sources of process modeling glare include the analyst's experience and the model's key stakeholders, project methodology, project constraints, elicitation techniques, tools, notations, the size and apparent complexity of the business being analyzed, and other interesting process dimensions.

Use the four-part Universal Business Process Definition to filter out glare and better perceive what others perhaps cannot see. Let's try on these "Business Process Sunglasses".

1) A business process is a repeatable collection of interrelated work tasks.

Identify one or more activities that comprise a business process. For example, what do we perceive as the set of activities that comprise an airline check-in process? We can probably observe activities such as: "finding a reservation, identifying the passenger, assigning seating, weighing the baggage, tagging the baggage, and depositing the baggage".

2) A business process is initiated by a business event.

Identify the logical boundary of where the process begins (and by exclusion, what does not cause the process to begin) by understanding a business process' initiating event. For example, what is the event that initiates the airline check-in process? How about, "When the passenger arrives at the counter or kiosk."? What is important is that the initiating event is identified.

3) A business process achieves an expected outcome.

Identify a business process' expected outcome(s). This is the logical boundary of where a process ends. More than a mere endpoint, an expected outcome is a reason for the process to exist, and it is the focus of the process' value-adding activities and flow. An expected outcome is not what a process produces, but why it produces it. When a business analyst elicits a process' expected outcome, he or she will understand why the process is performed. A process' outcome may be embodied in a tangible output, like a report or some form of data. But the expected outcome of a business process is more likely the content of the output. For example, the expected outcome of an Airport Check-in process may be that the passenger has received a boarding pass and checked his or her baggage. There may be several process inputs and outputs along the way to achieving these two expected outcomes of the Airport Check-in.

4) A business process is performed for a customer of the process.

Identify who or what will consume any of the business process' expected outcomes. For example, what or who are the consumers of the airline check-in process' outcome? Who or what needs or uses the boarding pass and the checked baggage that have been produced by this process?

Regardless of the type and scale of the business process being examined, the model's mission, resources, and project constraints imposed, use the four-part Universal Business Process Definition as your "business process sunglasses" to filter out the glare of unnecessary process observations. This will enable the business analyst to quickly perceive what other model stakeholders may not.

How to Normalize Any Business Process or Activity

Normalize any candidate business process or activity using the four-part Universal Business Process Definition.

A business analyst or process analyst need not ask a lot of questions to normalize a business process or workflow. They only need to ask a few focused questions (four in fact) and doggedly pursue and gain consensus about the four, sometimes-elusive, answers. The assumed basic structure of a business process will either be affirmed or restructured by the answers to the normalization questions.

Use the four-part Universal Business Process Definition to frame observations, and clarify the meaning of any candidate business process before the process is included in the business process model.

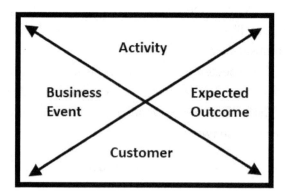

By answering four business process normalization tests throughout your elicitation and modeling, you will resolve ambiguity among stakeholders and organize business activities into optimal, modern business process, workflow, and activity structures.

Business Process Normalization Test 1:

Is the process a repeatable collection of interrelated work tasks? What are they?

A: Name one or more activities that comprise this business process.

Business Process Normalization Test 2:

Is the process initiated in response to a business event? What is it or what are they?

A: Identify what causes this business process to start.

Business Process Normalization Test 3:

Does the process have an expected outcome? What is it?

A: Name the expected outcome of this business process.

Business Process Normalization Test 4:

Does this process have a customer? Who is it or who are they?

A: Name who or what will consume the expected outcome of this business process.

If any of the four tests have not yet been satisfactorily answered, then the analyst will need to elicit more information (documentation reviews, interviews, workshops, mining) to satisfactorily answer the four process-defining tests.

Once all four tests have been sufficiently answered, the process has been normalized. Key ambiguities have been resolved, and a sound, fundamental business process structure has been established. Use the four answers to write a contextually accurate, unequivocal, plain-language process definition. No two processes will likely have the same definition within the same domain of analysis. The normalized process's defining structure will be the foundation of a contextually accurate, high-quality business process model, configured business procedure, or automated workflow.

UPMP Step 1 – Define the Process Model's Mission

Establish the intended use, tense, and required degree of abstraction of the business process model before investing significant modeling effort.

Some participants in a process modeling activity, like a workshop, may find themselves thinking or hearing any of the following comments:

- "I don't know why we're doing this. No one's going to use this model anyway."
- "This process just keeps expanding. At what point are we going to stop?"
- "This model is too general. It won't be useful."
- "This model is way too detailed. It won't be used."
- "We're just paving the cow paths here. We should be coming up with something brand new."
- "This is just pie in the sky. It doesn't reflect the real operation."
- "We're wasting time reviewing and revising unimportant details in the model."
- "Models? Why do we need models!"

By definition, any project is a unique and temporary endeavor. It has unique objectives, scope, project stakeholders, methodology or at least methodological rigor, opportunities, and constraints. Even projects that have similar modeling objectives, follow the same project methodologies and are expected to produce similar products have unique characteristics. They all have unique schedules and scopes. Some projects need process models to describe manual processes, while others need them to illustrate automated processes or software design. Some projects require a conceptual view of the business while others require logical or configuration views. Each project has its own unique set of stakeholders and each stakeholder has their unique point of view about what's important. Therefore, the model's mission and just what constitutes a high-quality business process model is unique to every project.

The purpose the mission produced in UPMP Step 1 will be to tailor and focus the remaining modeling activities and to validate the completed model's quality. This step should consume a relatively little amount (usually 1% to 3%) of the total time spent on process modeling. This is a small price to pay to improve the productivity and quality outcomes of the rest of the process modeling effort.

The benefits of a clear process model mission are improved productivity, improved quality, and reduced risk. Productivity will be improved because a clear mission will help the business analyst focus available time and effort on eliciting, defining, and refining only the process model components needed to complete the mission. A well-defined mission statement will provide clear quality criteria that enable the business analyst to assess whether the model is good enough to meet its intended use. A business process model's mission is a simple and inexpensive piece of insurance against risks that lead to effort and schedule overages or low model quality.

A high-quality business process model mission statement is the product of a concise model mission elicitation agenda. The answers to that agenda precipitate the mission statement content.

What you should learn about establishing a process model mission by reading this chapter:

- What comprises a high-quality business process model mission.
- Why a clear business process model mission is necessary.
- How to elicit the business process model mission using the three-part Universal Business Process Model Mission Elicitation Agenda.
- How to document the business process model mission in a few sentences of plain language.

Business Process Model Mission

A high-quality business process model mission specifies the business process model's intended use, tense, and required degree of abstraction.

A clear mission for the model will help to keep the modeling effort focused on what is important and what is not as the model is being developed. Its parameters can also be used to help validate the quality of the completed model.

An effective business process model mission should specify three key parameters:

1. **Whether the model will describe the process in its current or future state,**
2. **The model's intended use, and**
3. **The model's required degree of abstraction.**

Spending some effort to define a mission at the start of the modeling process is prudent and effective. It enables the business analyst to:

- Keep the forthcoming elicitation and modeling effort focused on what is important and avoid what is not. This, in turn, will help to keep the forthcoming elicitation efforts on track;
- Determine and choose the best-suited elicitation and modeling activities;
- Align or avoid conflicting stakeholder agendas and therefore avoid unnecessary frustrations and wasted effort;
- Create and maintain consensus among the project's key stakeholders about the model's intended use, tense, and degree of abstraction as the model is being developed;
- Define the parameters that can be used to assess model quality as it is being developed and before it is completed.

How to Elicit a Business Process Model Mission

Elicit the business process model mission using the three-part Universal Business Process Model Mission Elicitation Agenda.

Use the three-part Universal Business Process Model Mission Elicitation Agenda to establish a clear mission for a business process model. This agenda focuses initial elicitation on these three questions:

Universal Business Process Model Mission Elicitation Agenda Item 1:

What is the intended use of this model and who will use it?

A project's lifecycle has phases and constituent activities. A process model's intended use can be defined by identifying the project phase or activity that is expected to consume the model. For example, Six Sigma process improvement methodology calls for the use of process models among its Define, Measure, Analyze, Improve and Control phases. However, such project methodologies are often tailored, may only be loosely followed. They may even call for multiple process models (e.g., current state and future state process). Therefore, each process model's intended use should still be uniquely elicited and defined for each unique project.

The second part of eliciting the mission is to identify who will use this model. This can be answered with the name of the role that will perform the project phase or activity that will consume the model. When possible, it is even better to identify the person who will be performing that role, and therefore be aware of the personal expectations and capabilities of that person who is intended to consume the model.

Universal Business Process Model Mission Elicitation Agenda Item 2:

Will this model describe a business process in its current state or a future state?

Will this business process model describe a process as the process is being performed now, or as it will be performed in the future?

The answer is binary. Any single process model can only describe a business process in its current or future state.

Some project methodologies require two models: one model of the current process, followed by a second model of the future process. The current state process model is used as a baseline to identify where process changes or improvements could be made. The future process model describes what changes or improvements will be made.

Universal Business Process Model Mission Elicitation Agenda Item 3:

What is this model's required degree of abstraction?

Any model is by definition, an abstraction of the real world. How much abstraction Is suitable for the intended use and user of the model? This question can be effectively answered by one of three possibilities: conceptual, logical, or configuration (aka. physical).

Conceptual – A conceptual business process model has the highest degree of abstraction. It is a generalized view that communicates the process' defining characteristics and few if any other details. It is well suited for communicating a process' scope and key elements, like initiating event(s), expected succession of business activities, and expected outcome(s). Its intended audience is not seeking logical or physical (process configuration) details. Though it is a generalized view, a conceptual model still needs to be contextually accurate. Conceptual models are often illustrated using graphic notations other than BPMN because their intended audience is often non-technical managers or customers. For example, a conceptual scope diagram might use clip art instead of BPMN pools, and message flows that accurately illustrate what collaborations happen between a process and its external actors.

Logical – A logical view is perhaps the most commonly required degree of abstraction. It describes the details of interest to its intended reader without describing how the process is physically implemented in machines, procedures, or software configuration/coding. It will usually include process details such as activities, decision logic, assigned responsibilities, exceptions, delays, exchanges with external actors, process-related documentation, datasets, etc. In information technology methodologies, a logical degree of abstraction may illustrate requirements for, or the design of, software modules that are to be physically coded or configured. In business process management methodologies, a logical degree of abstraction may illustrate tasks, inputs, outputs, decisions, delays, exceptions, assigned responsibilities, etc. that are of interest to process control and optimization. In any case, a logical model needs to adhere to a modeling syntax, like BPMN, well enough for the model's reader to interpret the details correctly.

Configuration – A configuration business process model is a model of software modules, software workflow configuration, software program logic, machine components, or written procedures. It may communicate the physical configuration of physical machines, software modules, human operations, networks, files, messages, databases, documents, etc. Particularly when software workflow configuration or programming logic are being described, there is little or no margin for syntactical error in the model. The graphic elements in a configuration model describe what has been or is about to be configured or coded in software, physical devices, or written procedures. A configuration model needs to very closely adhere to a chosen modeling syntax, like BPMN.

Use these guidelines when deciding what the required degree of abstraction of a process model should be:

- Use conceptual process models to get agreement about and communicate <u>what</u> the process is. What is the scope? What causes it to be performed? What are the activities? What is the expected sequence of activities? What is or are the expected outcome(s)? Planning and scoping activities will typically use conceptual models.

- Use logical process models to communicate: How does or will the process work? Requirements gathering activities will typically require logical models because they specify contextually important details to a technical audience. What are the detailed tasks? Who does what?   What happens if...?   What happens when...?   What decisions will be made? What information is produced or used?

- Use configuration process models to communicate: What does the software code, machine/device, or person do? Software coding or process measurement activities will usually require exact physical details to instruct the software coder, describe a device or direct a person's activities.

Example

Most of us have traveled through airports. Let's consider the mission of a process model that will be developed for a project whose goal is to comply with new security regulations by changing how airline passengers are checked in for flights.

The elicitation agenda and answers about the model's mission could be:

Q: Universal Business Process Model Mission Elicitation Agenda Item 1:

What is the intended use of this model and who will use it?

A: This process model will be used by the airport operations manager to identify which standard operating procedures will need to be written or changed to meet new security requirements. This model will also be used by the change management team to summarize the new process in their training materials.

Q: Universal Business Process Model Mission Elicitation Agenda Item 2:

Will this model describe the process in its current state or its future state?

A: Produce a business process model of the future Airport Check-in process, to meet the new security requirements.

Q: Universal Business Process Model Mission Elicitation Agenda Item 3:

What is this model's required degree of abstraction?

A: The model will be used as an input to develop standard operating procedures that comply with the new no-fly registry and regulations. It will need to define enough logical details to develop standard operating procedures and training materials. A logical degree of abstraction is required.

How to Document a Business Process Model Mission

Document the business process model mission using a few sentences of plain language.

Document each business process model's mission statement in a few sentences of plain language. If you have followed the Universal Process Model Elicitation Agenda you should be able to state: a) the model's intended use, b) the required degree of abstraction, and c) if the model will describe the current or future (as-is or to-be) process. Assemble the three answers into a compound sentence or a very short paragraph.

You can structure a business process model mission statement using this simple pattern.

"Produce a *<conceptual, or logical or configuration>* business process model of the *<current or future>* *<process name>* business process(s)."

State who will use the model and what the model will be used for.

"This model will be used by *<name or role>* to *<activity or objective >*."

The result will be a concisely stated yet complete mission.

Example

Assembling the conclusions from the elicitation of the Airport Check-in business process model mission statement:

"Produce a logical business process model of the future Airport Check-in

process to comply with the new no-fly registry and regulations. This model will be used by the airport operations manager to identify which standard operating procedures to write or change and to train airline agents in the new check-in process."

The mission of a process model should be shared with the process model's key stakeholders: the modeling participants and its readers. Simply reiterate the mission in a brief "elevator speech" when starting the project, and restate the mission during remaining workshops, interviews, or other elicitation activities.

What is an "elevator speech"? If you encountered an executive in the elevator who asked you, "What is this model you're working on all about?", that executive should hear the same clear answer as the rest of the team. The response should be brief and clear enough to be given in the few seconds that it takes to ride an elevator. A few seconds is also all that's needed to focus an interview or workshop on the required tense, degree of abstraction (and justify the types of refinements required) to meet the intended use of the model by its intended user(s).

Exercise 1 – Define Business Process Model Mission

Review the notes provided to elicit the mission of the model and then document it.

Founded as an industrial chemical maker in Basel, Switzerland, in 1898, Chem AG is today a significantly diversified global manufacturer and distributor of industrial chemical products. Chem AG has significant multinational research and development, marketing, production, and distribution capability at its four plants located on four continents.

Chem AG relies on both regional and multinational suppliers for various raw and refined materials. For example, its research facility in Switzerland may need a very small amount (e.g. a few grams) of a specialized chemical compound, while a production plant in China may need relatively a large supply (1000 liters) of a common solvent. Another facility in Denver (located a thousand kilometers from the nearest ocean) may need a few pounds of sea sand.

Chem AG has hired you as a business analyst to participate in this important business and systems project. One of your responsibilities is to develop a business process model of Chem AG's business processes. You are to meet with the company's Chief Technology Officer soon to review your initial results.

Some initial information gathering has taken place.

Notes from an interview of H. Medelsky, President, two weeks ago:

Chem AG has prepared a business case wherein the expected benefits of this initiative are:

- Improve the efficiency and cycle time for purchasing materials by improving the integration between itself and registered/preferred suppliers;
- Standardize its purchasing process and systems across Chem AG's regional operating locations by using the same systems and process;

- Give registered suppliers the opportunity to compete on any Chem AG materials purchasing opportunities (not just regional ones), and all suppliers an even procurement playing field.

CACHE will be a digital solution through which any of Chem AG's facilities around the world will be able to request the supply of certain materials. Pre-qualified suppliers will bid to supply the materials. Chem AG's requesting facilities will be able to select the best bid received. This system should enable requests for materials to be decentralized, flexible, and timely, and enable the company to take advantage of suppliers around the world. The system will need to be integrated with Chem AG's existing centralized purchasing module of its SAP enterprise resource planning (ERP) system. The contract or purchase order and payment processes will be implemented as parts of the corporate enterprise business system, SAP.

The objective of the first stage is to document the scope and detailed requirements for this initiative. We need to identify what processes need to be implemented. We need to clarify how we'll manage suppliers and their bids. We need to define how we're going to standardize, and fairly and efficiently award bids for our projects. We also need to understand the responsibilities of CACHE, plant and purchasing managers so we can plan to manage changes.

By the end of this fiscal year, Chem AG expects to have developed and deployed on a pilot basis, its new Commodity Acquisition Clearing House/Exchange (CACHE) system. Based on the success of the CACHE pilot deployment this year, Chem AG has set a target for full deployment of the integrated system within one year. Based on the anticipated initial success, there is also the potential to license the use of the CACHE system to other large multinational SAP client companies, by the second year of operations.

The upcoming project phases will design, configure, test and deploy the digital solution and operational procedures. At the end of this first stage of the project, we expect your project team to give us a plan and budget estimate for the next stage.

What is this model's mission?

Use the Universal Business Process Model Mission Elicitation Agenda. Document your answer using a few sentences of simple language.

Compare your results to the proposed solution at www.ProcessModelingAdvisor.com.

UPMP STEP 2 – DEFINE SCOPE

Define the scope of a business process, as a named boundary.

A clear scope will help keep the remaining elicitation and modeling effort focused and on track. It will help a business analyst focus the modeling efforts on what is important. It will establish a consensus among the model's key stakeholders and a clear boundary about where to focus forthcoming modeling efforts. A clear scope is also crucial for meeting cost, schedule, and quality expectations for that model. Therefore, a business process model's scope should be defined before eliciting and documenting process flows, activities, and related details.

The purpose of UPMP Step 2 is to elicit and illustrate the model's scope - a named functional boundary around a set of one or more business processes and activities that are or will be included in the model. The activities that lie within that boundary need not yet be known or detailed. This named functional boundary can be illustrated using a scope diagram.

Though it might appear to be a simple drawing, a business process scope diagram is significant. It, along with the model's mission statement, is an important input for the elicitation of the rest of the model, including process flow(s), business activities, logical business process flow refinements, and validating the model's quality. A clearly defined business process scope establishes a foundation on which to elicit and build the business activities and flows that will comprise the model. In some larger projects, a process scope diagram can be one of the main artifacts at a project milestone. An elicited, documented scope, agreed among a project's key stakeholders may be one of the key outcomes of a large project's planning stage.

A clearly defined process model scope diagram will graphically communicate three important facts about the business process model.

They are:

1) **A named boundary:** a recognizable and acceptable name for the process whose details will be elaborated in the rest of the model;

2) **External actors:** the other processes, organizations, roles, and systems that surround the business process;

3) **Exchanges:** what is given or gotten between the process (at its boundary) and its external actors.

The key benefits of defining a business process model's scope are that it shows demonstrable progress early in the process modeling work, it is contextually valuable process documentation; it can be integrated with other business process model components or models; it can be easily communicated on one page, and it will focus the remaining elicitation and modeling efforts.

A process scope can be illustrated using a BPMN collaboration diagram. BPMN Pools depict the named boundary and the surrounding external processes, systems, organizations, and/or people with whom the process interoperates. BPMN Message Flows depict what the process logically gives and/or gets with the external actors.

What you should learn about business process model scope by reading this chapter:

- What business process scope is.
- Why a clearly defined business process scope is beneficial.
- How to elicit the business process model scope using the three-part Universal Business Process Scope Elicitation Agenda.
- How to illustrate business process scope using BPMN Pools and Message Flows in a BPMN collaboration diagram.

Business Process Scope

Business process scope is a named boundary around a set of activities, demarcated by what the process exchanges with its surrounding stakeholders.

Business process model scope is a named boundary of a group of related business activities. Business process model scope can be defined without yet knowing or detailing its constituent business processes and activities. This boundary is demarcated by what it exchanges with external actors. It defines what business activities do and do not lie within the boundary of the business process model, and therefore what should be the focus of the remaining business process analysis. The activities inside this boundary are or will be elaborated by the model's business process flow diagrams.

Business process model scope also defines what is not going to be elaborated on further in the model. The model will not elaborate on the details of any of the external actors: the other processes, systems, organizations, or persons that lie outside the scope boundary.

How to Elicit Scope

Elicit business process model scope using the three-part Universal Scope Elicitation Agenda.

The scope of any business process model can be established by eliciting the answers to three simple questions.

Use the three-part Universal Scope Elicitation Agenda along with the chosen elicitation technique(s) to establish a clear scope for any business process. The elicitation technique(s) that are chosen, the involvement of key stakeholders, and a clear mission for the business process model are also important dynamics in eliciting the scope "right". But this agenda is equally effective regardless of the elicitation techniques chosen, the model's mission, and the stakeholders involved at this point in a project.

The same scope elicitation agenda/questions should be posed and answered whether using workshop, brainstorming, conducting observations, etc. The business analyst can answer the questions or have a group answer them; they will need to be answered regardless of whether the model will be simple and small, or elaborate and large. The answers to these three questions will identify the defining elements of a process' scope: process name, external actors, and exchanges.

Universal Scope Elicitation Agenda Item 1:

What is the name of this process or function?

Every business process model depicts some scope of a business process or processes and that scope needs a recognizable name. The name should be familiar or agreeable to the modeling participants. That recognizable name should ideally imply the process' expected outcome. A couple of well-chosen words for a process model's name can summarize with clarity what has been or is about to be detailed throughout an entire process model, a standard operating procedure, or pages of system documentation.

A good, agreeable name may be elusive at the start of the analysis. The process model's full scope, constituent activities, and the expected outcome(s) have not yet been discovered. In this circumstance, the modeler should accept a suggestion that is at least familiar, if seemingly imperfect to the modeling participants. This name can be refined once the model has been at least essentially defined (in UPMP Step 3). Here are examples of some imperfect business process names:

1. The Colleague System
2. Landscape Analysis Tool
3. The *<company name withheld>* Company
4. Students Finance
5. Collision Data Interface
6. The Build Process

Be prepared to refine the name later in the model's development, once in-scope business flows, activities, initiating events, and expected outcomes and refinements become better understood. Ideally, a process model name will use a verb-subject pattern (i.e., communicate the expected outcome of the process), and be easily recognizable and meaningful to the model's reader. Here are names following a verb-subject pattern to replace the names initially proposed. The business process scope name implies the expected outcome (as general as each may be) of each process.

1. Administer Grants and Bursaries
2. Assess Landscape Sensitivities
3. Engineer and Market Networks
4. Award Student Funding
5. Exchange Collision Data
6. Generate Invoices

Universal Scope Elicitation Agenda Item 2:

Who or what are the external actors that surround this process or function?

With few exceptions, any business process needs to interact with something or someone that it serves or uses but that is outside its immediate control. In other words, the process interacts with external actors. A business process interoperates with external actors by requesting, receiving, or providing resources, services, and/or data to and from its external actors.

External actors can be types or sets of persons, organizations, systems, or even other processes. Two rules that distinguish external actors from the process with which they interoperate are:

1. External actors are not responsible for performing the process' activities.
2. A business process is not responsible for performing its external actors' activities.

External actors participate in the execution of a business process by giving the process something or getting something from it. But they do not perform or control the sequence of the process' activities.

For example, a credit card payment processing service is an external actor in a website's checkout process. Its activities are not controlled by the website, and they do not control the website although the credit card payment processing service is integral to completing checkout transactions. The credit card processing service will receive and verify a payment amount from the website's checkout process. The credit card processing service exchanges payment information with the website, and processes customer account and bank account transactions on behalf of the website. This example helps us to understand what an external actor is *not*. An external actor does not control the activities of a business process.

TYPES OF EXTERNAL ACTORS

A business process' external actors may be types of persons, organizations, automated systems, or other business processes.

Persons as external actors – Types of persons could be modeled as external actors to a business process. For example, a sales process exchanges information with a business's customers. Any individual customer is part of a class of external actors to the sales process, called "customer". A customer of the sales process is an external actor, because he or she is not responsible for performing the sales process' activities, but does participate by exchanging information (or other assets) with the sales process while it is executing.

Organizations as external actors – An organization could be modeled as an external actor to a business process. For example, a process that operates in a regulated business environment will likely involve a specific regulatory stakeholder. A pharmaceutical company's drug certification process would involve the exchange of information with, and the approval of, a federal regulatory agency.

Automated systems as external actors – An automated system could be modeled as an external actor to a business process. For example, a medical service provider's billing process could be designed to participate with accounting software such as general ledger and accounts receivable software.

Other Business Processes as external actors – One business process could be modeled as an external actor to another business process. For example, a medical service provider's billing process could be designed to exchange data with an accounting function, such as general ledger or accounts receivable functions of the accounting software package.

Universal Scope Elicitation Agenda Item 3:

What does this process or function give to or get from each of its external actors?

Once the process' external actors have been identified, you must also identify what each actor exchanges with the process. Exchanges may also be called "gives" and "gets", or "requests" and "responses". Whatever they are called, exchanges are typically some form of information, or another kind of resource, such as funding.

When eliciting exchanges between a process and the actors that surround it, open-ended questions are best: What does the business process give to or get from its external customers, suppliers, or governors (like a management function or regulatory agency)? Alternately stated: "What does the business process give to and get from any types of persons, organizations, automated systems, or other business processes?"

The answers to this type of question are typically nouns that may name either the media or the content of the exchange. If the model's required degree of abstraction is conceptual or logical, seek nouns that name the content of the exchanges, rather than the delivery media or mechanism. Some examples of nouns that name the content of the exchange include work request, credit approval, regulations, budget amount, account history, payment, maintenance schedule, etc. The names of exchanges in logical models are generally more qualified than in conceptual models. For example, "Customer Account History" is more qualified than simply, "Account History".

If the model's required degree abstraction is configuration, then expect to identify nouns that are physical media, or transport mechanisms for information or other assets between the business process and its external actors. Some examples of nouns that name physical media are: Work Ticket, Help Desk Call, Pick List, Check, Application Form, E-mail Notification. These may also be qualified by their expected content. For example: "Password reset Helpdesk Call, <xyz> Database Query, <xyz> Report, and <xyz> Form".

The business process' name, its external actors, and the process' exchanges with its external actors establish the model's scope or boundary. Later UPMP steps focus on the activities that lie within the named business process boundary, including those that produce or receive the message flows between the business process' boundary and its external actors.

Example

Let's return to our Airport Check-in business process, keeping the model's mission in mind:

"Produce a logical business process model of the future Airport Check-in process to comply with the new no-fly registry and regulations. This model will be used by the airport operations manager to identify which standard operating procedures to write or change and to train airline agents in the new check-in process."

The following notes have been elicited from a group of airline counter representatives using a workshop and the Universal Business Process Scope Elicitation Agenda. The elicitation notes and concluding answers to the agenda questions have been noted as follows:

Q: Universal Function Scope Elicitation Agenda Item 1:

What is the name of this process or function?

A: Airport Check-in.

Q: Universal Scope Elicitation Agenda Item 2:

Who or what are the external actors that surround this process or function?

A: Airline Ticketing System, Passenger, Airline Flight Operations System, Airport Baggage Handling System, and No-Fly Registry.

Q: Universal Scope Elicitation Agenda Item 3:

What does this process or function give to or get from each of its external actors?

A: Exchanges:

- Passenger *gives* passenger identification
- Passenger *gets* boarding pass and baggage claim tags
- Airline Ticketing System *gets* passenger identification
- Airline Ticketing System *gives* passenger reservation
- Flight Operations System *gives* flight manifest data
- Flight Operations System *gets* flight manifest update
- Baggage Handling System *gets* tagged baggage
- No-Fly Registry *gets* a no-fly inquiry
- No-Fly Registry *gives* a no-fly advisory

How to Illustrate Process Scope Using BPMN

Illustrate business process scope using BPMN Pools and Message Flows in a BPMN collaboration diagram.

A BPMN collaboration diagram can be used to effectively illustrate the scope.

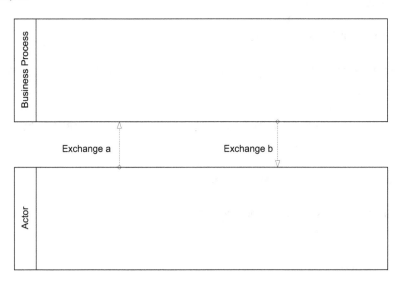

The business process that is the model's subject and each of its external actors are represented in a BPMN collaboration diagram as BPMN pools. The subject business process whose scope is being described is positioned as the central pool in the middle of the collaboration diagram, surrounded by other pools illustrating its external actors.

The exchanges ("gives" and "gets") that occur between the process (central pool) and its external actors (surrounding pools) are illustrated using BPMN Message Flows. BPMN Message Flows are used to illustrate what the business process exchanges with its surrounding external actors.

The details about the activities that lie within the central pool (business process) are now the focus of subsequent UPMP steps and model components, while the activities that lie within the external actors' pools will not be elaborated.

USING BPMN POOLS

Illustrate the business process and its surrounding actors (organizations, processes, persons and/or systems) using BPMN Pool flow objects.

BPMN Pool objects can be used to illustrate the scope of a business process and the boundaries of its surrounding external actors. The pool representing the named process is positioned in the middle of the diagram, surrounded by pools representing each of the external actors.

BPMN Pool Notation:

USING BPMN MESSAGE FLOWS

Illustrate the "gives" and "gets" between the business process and its surrounding actors using BPMN Message Flows.

BPMN Message Flow objects can be used to illustrate exchanges of an asset (typically information) that is given or gotten between one process and another. This includes any physical medium or logical information, or other assets that external actors give to or get from the business process.

BPMN Message Flow Notation:

An Arrow on a Dashed Line

From originating process or actor — — — Message Name — — — → To receiving process or actor

A BPMN collaboration diagram can be used to illustrate business process scope. BPMN Message flows can be used in a collaboration diagram to illustrate exchanges between the business process represented by the central BPMN Pool and the process' external actors (processes, systems, organizations, persons). Each message flow originates or ends at the boundary of each of two BPMN Pools. The message flow arrowhead indicates the flow's direction.

Example

Recall the scope information elicited about the Airport Check-in process. We can illustrate the scope that is elicited via the Universal scope elicitation agenda, using a BPMN collaboration diagram. We have a name for the process, the surrounding stakeholders, and the exchanges ("gives" and "gets").

Here is a BPMN collaboration diagram to illustrate the elicited Passenger Check-in business process scope information.

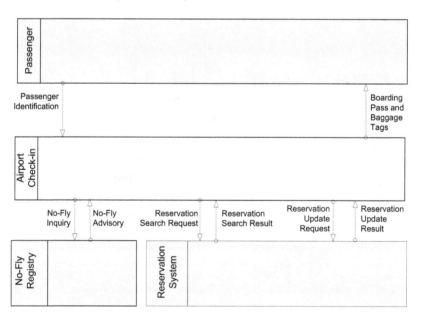

This BPMN collaboration diagram communicates a scope by illustrating the following:

1. The business process' boundary;
2. The business process' surrounding external actors; and
3. What the business process exchanges with its external actors.

This BPMN collaboration diagram clearly illustrates the Check-in Passenger process' boundary and the process' exchanges with its external actors.

The product of UPMP Step 2 is a scope diagram. It illustrates a named process boundary and exchanges with external actors. Because it illustrates a named boundary, a BPMN collaboration diagram can be used to focus on the remaining business process elicitation and modeling.

SCOPE MODELING TIPS

Look for Customers, Suppliers, and Controllers – When eliciting external actors, seek actors that play the roles of customers, suppliers, and controllers of the process. A customer is someone or something that requests a product or service with the expectation the request will be fulfilled. A supplier is someone or something that provides resources or services to the process to fulfill customer requests. A controller is an external actor that monitors or constrains the process.

Remember the 80/20 Rule – The 80/20 rule, or Pareto Principle, states that roughly 80% of effects come from roughly 20% of causes. Applied to process scope elicitation, you can expect to identify about 80% external actors and exchanges in this step and move on. Scope model refinements can come as part of subsequent modeling steps.

Exercise 2 – Define Scope

Review the notes provided to elicit the scope of the model and illustrate it using BPMN.

Notes from interview with E. Chow, Director – Enterprise Technology, two weeks ago:

We would like to build on the purchasing and accounts payable software and processes of our enterprise resource planning (ERP) system SAP. To make this new CACHE system fit, we want to make sure there are no overlapping responsibilities among systems and procedures.

Supplier companies, or more accurately their employees or representatives, will provide a profile and register as CACHE system users.

The Chem AG plant and process managers create Material Acquisition Requests (MARs) in SAP. They should not have to re-enter their MARs into the CACHE system. The CACHE system should receive approved MAR data (New, Add, Change) through a real-time interface with SAP.

Suppliers' users who have been activated in CACHE may sign on to the CACHE website, browse, and view posted RFQ information. They may create, update, and submit bids for selected RFQs.

Designated Chem AG users, such as purchasing managers and the plant managers, will be able to review and accept bids using the CACHE system.

Our SAP system will receive the accepted bid information from CACHE and we'll continue to use existing contracting, supplier management, accounts payable processes, and SAP for the rest of the procurement.

What is the scope of CACHE?

Use the Universal Business Process Scope Elicitation Agenda. Illustrate your answer using BPMN.

Compare your results to the proposed solution at www.ProcessModelingAdvisor.com.

UPMP STEP 3 – DEFINE BASIC BUSINESS PROCESS FLOW(S)

Establish the basic business process flow of each business process.

Think about all the houses in your neighborhood. They are all different, yet basically the same. Every one of them has the same basic structure: a foundation, walls, and a roof. If one lacks any of these basic elements, it is not a house. However, every house is also different, with unique details to suit the needs of its owner or occupants. One may be a bungalow, and another is a two-story. Some have attached garages, while others do not. Up the road may be a block of townhouses that from far away appears to be one home, but are, on closer inspection, several distinct homes.

Likewise, despite their scale or unique complexities or features all business processes have the same basic structural elements. They all can be perceived and modeled according to the same basic framework.

So far, in UPMP steps 1 and 2, we have elicited and documented a clear mission for the model and established a clear scope of the process model. The next step is to discover the one or more business process flows that lie within that scope. In UPMP Step 3 – Define Basic Business Process Flow(s), we will elicit and illustrate basic business process flows. The resulting basic process flow diagram(s) serves as the sound foundation for any further business process model elaboration and refinement. All process details and refinements will be built onto to this sound foundation.

Basic business process flow is the one or more initiating event(s) that cause anything to happen and a sequence of activities that lead to the process' expected outcome(s). Every business process has these basic elements, regardless of the process sale or complexity. This framework forms a sound and complete business process structure. Every high-quality business process flow diagram should include at least these basic elements.

The key benefit of establishing basic business process flow first is that it ensures that the process is at least fundamentally understood and framed. This provides benefits to all remaining process analysis and model refinement efforts, such as outcome orientation, productivity, syntactical quality, speed, demonstrable progress, reduced rework costs, model integration, fitness for use, knowledge foundation, flexibility, simplicity and clarity.

The basic business process flow elicitation agenda is focused on clarifying what the business process fundamentally is: What causes the process to begin? What is the expected sequence of activities? What is the process' expected outcome? These questions seem simple enough, but the answers may not be agreed upon or even apparent at the start of the analysis, particularly in large projects or enterprises.

Basic business process flow can be simply illustrated as a BPMN business process diagram (BPD), using BPMN event, activity, and flow objects. Because it will illustrate the essential elements of any process, a basic business process flow may be packaged along with the mission statement, scope diagram, and activity catalog as a conceptual business process model. Such a basic business process flow diagram is also easily integrated (both syntactically and contextually) into a larger and/or otherwise logically refined model.

What you should learn about basic business process flow by reading this chapter:

- That basic business process flow is the initiation and succession of business activities that lead to an expected outcome.
- That there are several clear benefits of establishing the basic business process flow.
- How to elicit the basic business process flow of any business process using the three-part Universal basic business process flow elicitation agenda.

- How to illustrate basic business process flow using BPMN start event, activity (task or sub-process), and end event flow objects.

Basic Business Process Flow

Basic business process flow always includes the initiation and succession of business activities that lead to an expected outcome.

Too many business process models lack even basic business process flow elements. For example, many not so high-quality process models start at a point called "Start", which is meaningless, or with an activity. Basic flow includes the contextually meaningful initiation, sequence of activities, and expected outcome of a business process.

Basic business process flow includes three contextually essential elements:

1. **Initiation** – the business event that initiates the process;

2. **Expected Activity Sequence** – the expected sequence of activities (at least one) that are executed in response to the event; and

3. **Expected Outcome** – the expected outcome of the process.

The basic elements of any business process, its Initiating event, expected activity sequence, and expected outcome, illustrated in a basic business process flow diagram, are togeher the contextual and graphical framework upon which all further business process flow refinements will be made.

How to Elicit Basic Business Process Flow

Elicit basic business process flow using the three-part Universal Basic Business Process Flow Elicitation Agenda.

Every business process must have a reason to start. This reason is its initiating event. Once started, the process' activities are performed in an expected sequence. Every business process has some expected outcome, typically for that process' customer. These basic business process characteristics can be defined for any business process regardless of process scale and complexity, from the most complex to the simplest, regardless of whether a process is understood at its most generalized or detailed level. These basic elements are always elicited using the same Universal Basic Business Process Flow Elicitation Agenda.

Each of these three agenda items is described below:

Universal Basic Business Process Flow Elicitation Agenda Item 1:

What causes this process to start?

A good place to start eliciting a business process flow is at its beginning. Some incident or change in the real world prompts the process to begin. This happening can be thought of as an event. What specifically is it?

The answer to what causes a business process to start will most often fall into one of these common categories:

- The process is initiated by an **input or request.** An incoming message is received from an external actor or another process. What is it?
- The process is initiated by a **schedule**. A point in time or time interval occurs. What is it?
- The process is initiated by a **responsibility hand-off**. The responsibility for doing work shifts from one person, organization, or system to another. What is it?
- The process is initiated by a **business rule or policy**. A condition that is defined by a business policy or rule becomes true. What is it?

- The process is initiated by an **error or exception.** A predictable, periodic exception to another process' normally expected flow happens. What is it?

Starting basic business process flow elicitation with the first question, "What causes this business process to start?" has a number of benefits:

- It clarifies **why** a business process exists. Even if the set activities that comprise a business process are not yet clear, an understanding of what causes it to begin validates that the process has a reason to exist. *For example, without knowing any of the details about the activities that comprise an ATM transaction, it is clear an ATM process needs to exist if we can see what causes it to begin. We can be confident that further process details can be uncovered.*
- It helps to clarify the **scope** of a business process. Knowing what causes a business process to start defines a boundary of the process. The remaining elicitation and modeling can focus on what happens after, not before, the initiating event. *For example, in the case of an ATM transaction, we know that issuing an ATM card is not part of the scope of an ATM transaction, but part of another process. So, the analysis of the ATM transaction process need not include that in its scope.*
- It can also clarify how a process can **interact** with other processes or process stakeholders. Business processes may be linked through events, where the outcome of one business process is the initiating event of another. What causes one process to start may be the outcome reached by another process.

Examples

Here are some examples of initiating events that cause business processes to start:

- Inserting a card starts an ATM process. (Card Inserted)
- A customer phones a call center, causing the call event management process to begin. (Customer Call Received)

- The end of the month causes the invoicing process to begin. (Month End)
- The quantity of an inventory item on-hand is below the reorder limit, causing the inventory reorder process to begin. (Reorder Level Reached)
- A project is over budget, causing a review process to begin. (Project Over Budget)
- The last deliverable of a project has been completed, causing the administrative closure process to begin. (All Deliverables Completed)
- Sometimes, what causes a business process to begin is a combination of conditions:
  - At the end of a fiscal month, the actual current month sales are less than the current target for month sales. Because it is the end of the month AND actual sales are lower than target, the marketing effectiveness review process begins. In this example, both conditions need to be true for the process to begin. (Sales Below Target)
  - A project is more than 20% under budget, OR it is more than 15% over budget, OR the forecasted end date is later than the planned end date, AND it is the end of the month, so the review process starts. In this example, only one of the conditions separated by the OR conjunction, along with the end-of-month condition, need to be true for the process to begin. (Project Out of Limits)

Universal Basic Business Process Flow Elicitation Agenda Item 2:

What happens next?

(Once answered, the question is repeated.)

Once a business process begins, its activities (at least one) are executed in logical succession, or a "flow", towards achieving the expected outcome. Eliciting the expected sequence or "flow" is mostly a matter of identifying successive activities. Once completed, each activity has a successor. Its successor will typically be a) the next business activity that contributes towards achieving this process's expected outcome, or b) this process' expected outcome will have been reached.

The most effective way to elicit and uncover the "flow" is to simply ask or observe, "What happens next?" Even if the answer seems obvious, asking the question has at least a few benefits.

In any workshop or interview, ask the open-ended question "What happens next?" followed by silence. Waiting for an answer encourages stakeholders to engage and think of an answer to fill that uncomfortable silence.

Asking "What happens next?" is a simple and easy step-by-step modeling approach. It focuses on identifying candidate business activities one at a time, in a logical progression

Asking "What happens next?" begs an answer rather than imposing one. Asking this simple question encourages the stakeholders involved in the elicitation to propose their input to the answer.

Listening or observing, instead of imposing, is the way to get the "right" answer. Listening for and taking modeling participants' answers gives them a personal stake in the model's content. Because it's their answer they don't need to be convinced that it's that right, or at least a very good proposition for the model.

Universal Basic Business Process Flow Elicitation Agenda Item 3:

What is the expected outcome of this process?

All good things come to an end, including business process flows. According to the Universal Business Process Definition, every business process or activity has an expected outcome.

A process' expected outcome(s) may not be clear or agreed upon at the start of its elicitation. Some processes produce several outputs on the way to achieving their expected business outcome. A process may reach an alternate outcome or even be aborted before reaching its expected outcome. Process outputs or alternate outcomes can be elicited, as process model refinements, once the expected outcome has been established. Every business process must have an expected outcome.

There are several obvious benefits to establishing and knowing the expected outcome at the outset. It demarcates the expected endpoint of a business process. Knowing the expected outcome focuses subsequent elicitation on those activities and decisions needed to achieve that outcome. Knowing the expected outcome also causes business activities that do not contribute to that outcome to be called into question or discarded. Together with the initiating event, the expected outcome clearly defines a boundary for the business process flow, even if the activities and logical details that will occur between them are not yet refined.

Example

Let's return again to the Airport Check-in business process.

A passenger checking in for a flight at the airport could describe her own experience and her observations of other passengers:

- A passenger arrived at the check-in counter or kiosk.
- The passenger identified himself to the airline representative or kiosk (by presenting a passport, picture identification, or credit card used to make the reservation).
- The airline representative or kiosk found the passenger's reservation and verified the passenger's identity.
- The airline representative or kiosk made, confirmed, or changed the passenger's seat assignment.
- The airline representative or kiosk issued baggage tags for each of the passenger's checked bags.
- The airline representative or kiosk issued the passenger a boarding pass.
- The airline representative weighed each of the passenger's checked bags.

- Once the passenger was issued a boarding pass and baggage tags, the airline representative or the passenger transferred the passenger's tagged baggage onto the airport's baggage conveyor and the check-in process ended.
- The passenger left the check-in area and moved on to security.

Using our common observations as airline passengers and the Universal Basic Business Process Flow Elicitation Agenda, let's establish the basic business process flow of the Airport Check-in process.

Q: Basic business process flow Elicitation Agenda Item 1:

What causes this business process to start?

A: Passenger arrives at a check-in kiosk or counter.

Q: Basic business process flow Agenda Item 2:

What happens next?

A: Find Reservation.

(Once answered, the question is repeated.)

What happens next?

A: Verify Passenger Identity, Assign Seating, Check Baggage, Issue Boarding Pass and Baggage Tags.

Basic business process flow Agenda Item 3:

What is the expected outcome of this business process?

A: Boarding Pass Issued and Baggage Tags Issued.

The Universal Basic Business Process Flow Elicitation Agenda focuses modeling participants on establishing a consensus about the key elements that define a process. It is concise and focused, so it expedites and simplifies elicitation.

The answers to this simple agenda are not always easy to agree on. Especially when there are several stakeholders involved in the elicitation. For example, checking in at an airport seems to be a common enough experience for us all. However, there will initially be many different opinions about where the Airport Check-in business process starts and ends, and its order of activities. Some might say it begins when we simply walk up to the counter or kiosk. Some might say it starts when a passenger purchases a ticket.

This focused Universal Basic Business Process Flow Elicitation Agenda avoids the digressions about details that could be interesting but are beyond essential business process flow characteristics. Instead, it establishes the sound foundation upon which all types of refinements can be added.

In the Airport Check-in example, could more activities occur? Could more details about the process be added? What would happen if the passenger wanted to change seat assignments? What would happen if the passenger were on a no-fly list? What is the difference if any, between checking in at an automated kiosk or online rather than with an airline representative? What would happen if the bags were over the acceptable weight? The list of possible refinements could go on and on. These and other refinements should be deferred because they can be efficiently elicited and added to the model during UPMP Step 5 – Refine Business Process Flow(s), on the sound foundation that has been established here.

How to Illustrate Basic Business Process Flow Using BPMN

Illustrate basic business process flow using BPMN start event, activity (task or collapsed sub-process), and end event Flow Objects.

According to the standard published by Object Management Group (www.omg.org):

"In BPMN a Process is depicted as a network of Flow Objects, which are a set of activities and the controls that sequence them."

According to the Universal Business Process Definition, every business process is initiated in response to an event. It includes at least one business activity and has an expected outcome. So, to be complete, every business process flow diagram, draft or final, basic or refined, at any level of detail or degree of abstraction, should graphically depict at least those three basic business process flow elements.

Any business process's initiating event and sequence of activities that lead to the expected outcome(s) are illustrated using just a few BPMN graphical elements: start event, sequence flow, task, and end event.

Every basic business process flow diagram illustrates what causes the process to start. This is illustrated using a BPMN start event.

- **BPMN Start Event** graphically illustrates why a process is initiated. Use a BPMN Start Event object to illustrate the initiation of any business process flow.

In a basic business process flow diagram, the start event triggers a sequence of one or more business activities. Illustrate the succession of business activities using BPMN sequence flows and BPMN tasks.

- **BPMN Sequence Flow** graphically depicts the succession of events, activities, and other elements (e.g., decisions) of a process. Use BPMN Sequence Flow objects to illustrate the expected sequence or "flow" of activities and other elements from the initiating event through to the expected outcome of a business process.
- **BPMN Task** graphically depicts an activity that is not comprised of other activities in the model. Use BPMN Task objects to illustrate business activities whose composition are not, at least not yet, detailed elsewhere in the business process model

Every business process has an expected outcome. Its basic business process flow diagram depicts process's expected outcome using a BPMN end event.

- **BPMN End Event** graphically depicts where a business process ends. Use a BPMN End Event object to illustrate the expected outcome of a business process.

Note: BPMN offers specialized objects for illustrating specialized start event and end event sub-types. Refer to Appendix 2 Using BPMN Start Event and End Event Sub-Types for examples of BPMN's specialized start event and end event subtypes.

Even in its simplest form, any business process can be illustrated in the same syntactically complete, basic way.

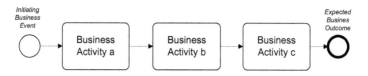

A business process can be most simply diagrammed as a single task that is bounded by its start and end events.

Though highly generalized, this model is still contextually and syntactically complete.

Example

Recall the basic business process flow information that was elicited about the Airport Check-in process. Here's a basic business process flow diagram of the Airline Check-in process using BPMN.

This BPMN business process flow diagram communicates that the event Passenger Arrives for Check-in initiates a set of related activities in an expected sequence to achieve the expected business outcome.

Even the simplest basic business process flow diagram of the Airport Check-in process includes the contextually important information that defines this business process: that the Airline Check-in process is initiated in response to an event (Passenger Arrives for Check-in) that achieves an expected outcome (Passenger Issued Boarding Pass).

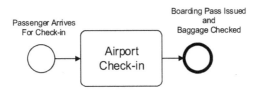

This simple Airport Check-in business process flow diagram is syntactically complete and consistent with other process flow diagrams in the model. Though super-summarized, it is contextually accurate. It can be easily understood. It can be integrated into a larger business process model. Such a highly summarized view can be useful when:

1. The details about how this process's expected outcome is achieved may be hidden or do not need to be communicated to the intended audience.
2. Its details will be elicited later in the model's development. Until then, this basic business process flow diagram scopes and depicts a placeholder for that process in the greater model.

ILLUSTRATING PARALLEL ACTIVITIES
But what if what happens next is two or more concurrent activities?

Illustrate parallel activities as two or more concurrent flows using a BPMN AND Fork gateway and eventually merge them back into one using a BPMN AND Merge gateway.

When what happens next is two or more concurrent business activities, use a BPMN AND Fork Gateway to illustrate parallel, concurrent activity flows.

If parallel flows are created, then eventually, the parallel flows must converge. An AND Fork must be followed by a companion BPMN AND Merge Gateway somewhere in the succeeding process flow to illustrate that point in the process flow where the parallel flows converge back into a single flow.

EXAMPLE

While boarding a commercial airline flight, many of us passengers have observed that a flight's baggage is also being loaded while the plane is being boarded. The Load Baggage and the Board Passengers activities are being performed at the same time – in parallel, not in sequence. Once all the passengers are boarded and the baggage has been loaded onto the plane, the plane leaves its gate. The Load Baggage activity is often complete before all the passengers have boarded, but not always. In some instances, all the passengers may be boarded, but the first officer or captain will announce that the fight is still waiting for a few more connecting passengers' luggage to be loaded onto the plane. Either way, the plane will only leave the gate once both those activities have been completed.

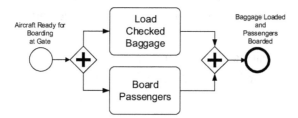

Basic Business Process Flow Modelling Tips

A business process may be composed of multiple process flows.

Business analysts suppose that all the in-scope activities that they discover must be contained within one sequential business process flow. But, a sound, modern business process structure is more likely comprised of several distinct business process flows.

In the following example, the Accept, Index and Serve Content business process is comprised of three distinct business process flows, that are themselves distinguishable, sound business processes. They each have their distinct initiating event, followed by one or more business activities, that lead to an expected outcome. Each stands the test of the Universal Business Process Definition and business process normalization tests.

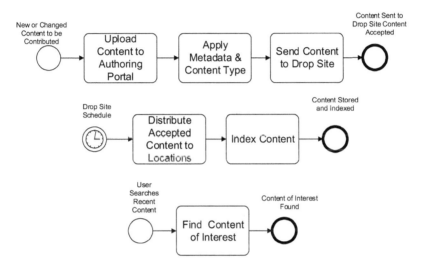

Update the scope diagram and activity catalogue as business process flows are being defined. It is good practice to review and update the scope diagram as basic business process flow(s) are elicited and discovered. The initial scope diagram may have omitted some exchanges or external actors that are now found to be the initiating events of in-scope business process flows.

Focus the flow on what leads to the expected outcome. Focus basic process flow elicitation on the expected sequence of business activities that will achieve the expected outcome. Avoid diverging into alternate or exception flows, decomposition, business decision logic, or other refinements. Elicitation of logical refinements is important, but they are not needed to establish basic process flow and they will slow down the initial elicitation and modeling. UPMP Step 5 – Refine Business Process Flow(s) will elicit and illustrate refinements.

80/20 Rule – 80% of basic business process flow can often be elicited during the first 20% of the total modeling effort. The basic process flow is a sound structural foundation that can be identified quickly by asking a few, right questions. The remaining 80% of process modeling will be spent adding logical refinements, reviewing and validating the model. In all but the simplest models, business process modeling is a journey of discovery. Like any other structure, a model will be refined and elaborated further once it is outlined. For example, once the basic process flow is defined, the analyst may use it to plan follow-up workshops or other forms of elicitation with their own agendas to elicit refinements.

Sometimes, a basic business process flow diagram is all that's needed to meet the model's mission. A basic business process flow may be the only diagram that's needed to meet the model's mission. If the intended use of the model is planning and the required degree of abstraction is conceptual, a basic business process flow diagram may be all that's needed, without pursuing further logical refinements, like decomposition, decision logic, etc. Exercise 3 – Define Basic Business Process Flow(s)

Review the notes provided to elicit the basic business process flow(s) of CACHE and illustrate it using BPMN.

Notes from a teleconference with Manfred Weiss, SAP Operations Manager, and Naveen Lawande, Applications Team Leader, one week ago:

To be able to perform CACHE's key supplier functions, suppliers' employees or representatives will need to register as CACHE supplier users.

- A new user's email address will be used as their CACHE userid.
- Supplier user profile data will need to be entered and saved.
- CACHE will also send the Chem AG procurement department (via email) a notification that the new userid and profile have been created.

- When the Chem AG procurement department receives the email notification it will activate the new CACHE user.
- SAP will send approved MARs to CACHE. Each MAR will have already been created and approved within the SAP system.
- When the CACHE system receives a MAR it will create a Request for Quotation (RFQ) for each item contained within the MAR.
- It will post new RFQs into its database.
- CACHE will also email RFQs in PDF format to any suppliers whose profiles match the material types contained in the RFQ.

Active suppliers who log in to the CACHE system will be able to browse all the current RFQs that have not expired or closed. Here they will be able to select and view an existing RFQ.

Suppliers may create, update, and submit bids for selected RFQs. A bid will include information about the commodity price and quantity, delivery method, price, delivery from and to locations, and delivery date.

- The system should automatically identify current Export/Import customs duties and calculate the duties.
- The system should also automatically identify special handling requirements and any environmental duties based on the commodity and include that information in the suppliers' bid.
- Suppliers may also view a previously saved bid and update that bid until it is submitted.
- Once a bid is submitted, CACHE will send a notification to the project manager who submitted the MAR.

Once the supplier submits their bid, it cannot be changed, and it is stored in the system until the RFQ's time limit has expired or one bid has been accepted.

Daily, CACHE will archive and purge expired bids.

Chem AG purchasing managers and the plant/project managers will regularly review and accept bids. They will review the schedule, cost, environmental duties, etc. of bids. They will be able to accept the bid that they prefer.

Once a bid is accepted by both a purchasing manager and a plant manager it can move on to contracting. Once the two reviewers have accepted a single bid, the CACHE system will close the RFQ and send the accepted bid data to the SAP system. The accepted bid data will contain the original MAR data, supplier ID, and other bid information. CACHE will also archive the RFQ and all bids received. That's basically where the responsibilities of the CACHE system will end.

When the SAP system receives accepted bid information from CACHE, SAP will look up the supplier profile and the material acquisition request, determine if there is a supplier agreement in place or if one needs to be created, determine what other procurement steps need to be completed, and notify the purchasing department contact identified on the MAR. The purchasing department contact will proceed with the remaining procurement management activities (contract management, supplier management, and accounts payable activities) using SAP and other established procedures.

What is/are the basic process flow(s) within the CACHE process?

Use the Universal Basic Business Process Flow Elicitation Agenda. Illustrate your answer using BPMN.

Compare your results to the proposed solution at www.ProcessModelingAdvisor.com.

UPMP STEP 4 – DEFINE BUSINESS ACTIVITIES

Define the business activities that comprise the business process.

A high-quality business process model includes clear, unambiguous business activity definitions, that can be clearly communicated and validated among the model's key stakeholders. Not only are unequivocally defined business activities building blocks of sound business process structures, but they have the best potential to be re-used among different processes within the same business domain.

Business analysts often have these questions about how to define their models' business activities.

- How should I perceive the business activities that comprise a business process?
- How should I clearly distinguish and justify where one activity ends and another activity begins?
- To what level should I decompose the activities into sub-activities?
- When and why will it make sense to break one activity into two? When should I combine two or more activities into one?
- How can I write a meaningful, unambiguous business activity definition?

As a result, most business process models lack activity definitions altogether or have activity definitions that are not very useful to or are even misinterpreted by the model's intended users.

UPMP Step 4 resolves all this ambiguity. The purpose of UPMP Step 4 is to define the business activities that were identified in UPMP Step 3, or that may be discovered through model refinements in UPMP Step 5. In this step, the analyst will review the candidates, normalize and unequivocally define the model's business activities, according to the Universal Business Process Definition, using the Business Process Normalization technique. That is accomplished through a clear and focused business activity elicitation agenda. This will lead to clarity and unequivocal definition of each candidate activity in the model, regardless of the elicitation technique(s) chosen or the model's required degree of abstraction.

This step will produce an Activity Catalogue that will be the model's text-based reference or glossary about the business activities that appear in the process flow diagrams.

The benefits of taking this step include quality, consistency, efficiency, flexibility, and the opportunity for reuse. Clearly defining the activities will reduce the likelihood of rework as the model's process flows are refined. When all business activities in the model have been unambiguously defined, all associated specifications such as written operating procedures, use cases, or other design specifications, can also be squarely developed. Defining or clarifying the meaning of business activities saves time. Well-defined business activities have a good chance to be reused in more than one business process flow, and therefore become reusable services within a system or set of business operations.

What you should learn about defining business activities by reading this chapter:

- How to elicit business activity definitions using the Universal Business Process Definition.
- How to normalize and clearly define any candidate business activity using the four-part Universal Business Process Definition.
- How to document all business activities in an Activity Catalogue, and give every activity a clear name and definition.

Business Activity

Clearly define any business activity according to the four-part Universal Business Process Definition.

So, what is a business activity? Any business activity is just another business process. It just happens to be used within a larger process. Any activity is initiated in response to an event. It is comprised of one or more tasks. It achieves an expected business outcome for one or more customers of the process.

Any activity is definable in the same way as any process is definable, according to the four-part Universal Business Process Definition. A competent business analyst will apply the Universal Business Process Definition (i.e., wear their business process sunglasses) to perceive, normalize or define any business activity, regardless of how the activity is elicited, its scale, its apparent simplicity or complexity, or where the activity appears in a larger process.

How to Elicit and Define Business Activities

Elicit business activity definitions using the two-part Universal Business Activity Definition Agenda.

The conventional questions that could be asked to elicit business activity definitions seem credible enough, such as:

- What activities are required to transform process inputs into process outputs?
- What is the functional decomposition of the larger activities sub-activities, or tasks?
- What are the steps or activities that add value to transforming customer requests into satisfied customer requests?

Each of these questions will prompt an answer. But in practice, they are prone to produce unclear or widely inconsistent. They are too simple and unqualified to sufficiently elicit and establish a sound, unequivocal understanding the purpose and boundaries of any activity in the business process model.

Use the two-part Universal Business Activity Elicitation Agenda to understand and define all business activities in the business process model:

Universal Business Activity Definition Agenda Item 1:

What are (name) the candidate business activities?

Identify candidate business activities by reviewing the existing business process flow diagram. Use either the basic business process flow diagram produced in UPMP Step 3 or the refined diagram(s) produced in UPMP Step 5.

If no process flow diagram exists and only a scope diagram exists (the product of UPMP Step 2) then it is possible to infer candidate business activities from the scope diagram. The scope diagram identifies incoming and outgoing exchanges. Identify one candidate business activity to receive each incoming message flow and one to produce each outgoing message flow. There would be as many candidate business activities as the sum of incoming and outgoing exchanges on the scope diagram. For example, a courier or postal worker delivers mail to the company mailroom. This incoming exchange indicates a business activity, like Receive Mailroom Mail. Or an outgoing exchange happens when a student is sent a notification that she has been registered for a course. This exchange indicates a business activity, like Send Course Registration Notification.

Universal Business Activity Definition Elicitation Agenda Item 2:

Does each candidate business activity pass the four-part Universal Business Process Definition?

An activity's name identifies it, but its initiating event, set of activities, expected outcome, and customer define it. Use the four-part Universal Business Process Definition to normalize and define each candidate business activity. This testing is not a test in the sense of measuring your knowledge. It is an agenda for eliciting and discovering meaning producing sound, clear activity definitions. If a candidate activity does not pass one of the tests, more elicitation is required to refine its meaning.

How to Define Candidate Business Activities

Define any candidate business activity using the four-part Universal Business Process Definition.

A high-quality business process model contains clearly defined business activities. A business activity that has been identified in a workshop or other type of elicitation could be a valuable concept that may be in-scope, may have a good activity name (using a verb-subject pattern), and may sound familiar and agreeable. But, despite its name, its meaning is still open to interpretation by the model's reader.

Here are the four "tests" to apply to each candidate business activity:

Activity Test 1:

Is it a repeatable collection of related work tasks? What are they?

This is the easiest test to apply to any candidate business activity. Normally, some sub-activities or tasks can be named without much thought. The analyst should be able to further envision or list at least some sub-activities that comprise a business activity, even if it is not necessary to document those details to meet the modeling mission. It might be that no meaningful work tasks can be identified or its tasks wholly duplicate that of another activity in the model (i.e., it is an alias of another activity). In such cases, a candidate activity will need to be re-examined or even discarded.

Activity Test 2:

Is it initiated in response to a business event? What is it or what are they?

The business analyst should be able to identify what causes the business activity to start. What is its initiating event? A business activity may be initiated when another activity's outcome has been achieved, when a request has been made of it by another activity, or when some periodic business condition or rule becomes true. If candidate business activity is found in a process flow diagram, then its initiating event is likely the expected outcome of its predecessor in the flow.

Activity Test 3:

Does it have an expected outcome? What is it?

The analyst should be able to name the expected outcome of the business activity. Does it have an expected outcome? Just like business processes, any business activity must have an expected outcome. The expected outcome is usually an incremental outcome of the larger business process to which the activity belongs.

Activity Test 4:

Who or what is its customer?

A: The business analyst should be able to name who or what will consume the expected outcome of this business activity. Often, the consumer of an activity's outcome is its immediate successor in the flow.

Example

Recall the basic business process flow diagram of the Airline Check-in process that was produced in UPMP Step 3:

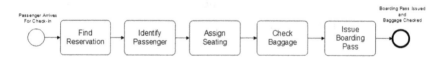

Reviewing the Airport Check-in process and using the Universal Business Process Definition, let's ask and answer the Universal Business Activity Definition Elicitation Agenda questions.

Elicitation Notes:

Q: Business Activity Elicitation Agenda Item 1:

What are (name) the candidate business activities?

A: The basic business process flow diagram produced in UPMP Step 4, candidate business activities are:

- Find Reservation,
- Identify Passenger,
- Assign Seating,
- Check Baggage, and
- Issue Boarding Pass.

Here is an example of how to define one of the candidate business activities using the Universal Business Process Definition:

Find Reservation

Activity Test 1: Is it a repeatable collection of interrelated work tasks? What are they?

Yes. Find Reservation requires searching the reservation system for the person who has arrived for check-in and finding a match for their expected itinerary.

Activity Test 2: Is it initiated in response to an event? What is it or what are they?

Yes. Find Reservation is initiated by presenting or scanning, at the counter or kiosk, an acceptable piece of personal identification, entering a reservation code, or scanning the credit card that was used to make the reservation.

Activity Test 3: Does it achieve an expected outcome? What is it?

Yes. The expected outcome of Find Reservation is that the passenger's reservation has been found and her/his related flight ticketing, retrieved from the reservation system.

Activity Test 4: Who or what is its customer?

The customers of the Find Reservation business activity are any of the rest of the Airport Check-in activities: Identify Passenger, Assign Seating, Check Baggage, and Issue Boarding Pass. They all consume the itinerary information that was found and confirmed by Find Reservation.

Business Activity Elicitation Guidelines

Here are some practical elicitation guidelines to keep in mind when eliciting candidate business activities.

Review the Mission Statement – Briefly review the business process model's mission statement before starting to elicit candidate business activities. Review whether the model is to include only current or also future activities, the model's required degree of abstraction (conceptual, logical, or configuration), who will use the model, and what they are expected to use it for.

Review the Basic Business Process Flow Diagram – The basic business process flow diagram produced in UPMP Step 3 already identifies candidate business activities.

Use the Scope Diagram – If there is no basic business process flow diagram, use the exchanges (message flows) on the scope diagram produced in UPMP Step 2, to identify candidate business activities. Identify one candidate business activity for each exchange on the scope diagram. Name one activity for each in-scope requests and responses.

Avoid Deep-Dives – Avoid/Defer eliciting details such as activity decomposition, decision logic and exception handling activities. These will be addressed in UPMP Step 5.

Look for Activity Indicators – Whenever new candidate business activities are proposed, then discover why. As the model is being refined, new candidate business activities might be proposed whenever there is a responsibility hand-off, error condition, input received, output produced, business rule, or work schedule.

Don't Work in Isolation – Competent business analysts avoid working in isolation. Your perception is only one of many stakeholders' realities. Even if you have answers, also having other stakeholders' answers is important. Use workshops or interviews to engage key stakeholders in candidate business activity elicitation.

How to Document Business Activities

Give each activity a clear name and definition.

An Activity Catalogue is part of a high-quality business process model. It can be documented in various forms. In its simplest form, the Activity Catalogue may be a list produced during a workshop or interview. An Activity Catalogue can be easily recorded in a document or spreadsheet. Most process modeling software will include some form of a database with the capability to record additional activity characteristics and provide multiple views or reports about the activities' data.

Regardless of the tool and format used to document it, a business process model's Activity Catalogue will describe at least two important characteristics of each business activity: a unique name and a clear, meaningful, and unequivocal definition.

Activity Name – An activity name that uses the imperative voice (verb-subject pattern), implies the activity's expected outcome, and uniquely distinguishes that activity from all other activities in the model.

Activity Definition – an activity definition that answers the four-part Universal Business Process Definition using clear and relevant language. Once the activity has been normalized, its four-part definition will be unequivocal - unique within the domain of the model.

Once an activity is uniquely named and defined, other activity attributes or documents can be attached to it in the Activity Catalogue. Activity-relevant attributes can include related policy documents, use cases, test cases, standard operating procedures, performance measurements, and model configuration management attributes:

- Use cases may describe the design of software that implements the activity;
- Test cases may describe the testing that will be performed to validate the activity or software that implements the activity;
- Standard operating procedures may describe the procedure to be followed to perform the activity.
- Performance measurement attributes – such as modeled or actual cycle times, defects, and cost data.
- Configuration management (revision history metadata) attributes – such as version, date, who made the update, etc. of the Activity Catalogue or specific activity definitions.

Consider a project's overarching methodology, the mission of the model, the modeling tools at hand, and your organization's accepted standards to determine what other activity attributes to include in the Activity Catalogue.

ACTIVITY NAME
Establish meaningful business activity names using a verb-subject pattern.

Coming up with a simple, unambiguous business activity name that can be consistently interpreted across an organization seems like a tall order. But clearly, it can be done. Just a couple of words, in a simple verb-subject pattern, can stand on their own as a meaningful, imperative sentence. For example, Pay Cashier likely has the same general meaning for nearly everyone. Why? A good business activity name uses a verb-subject pattern. Even the simplest process or activity name should be a minimum of two words – a verb and a subject. In the same way that a simple, well-written sentence can tell an entire story, the imperative verb-subject pattern has a good chance of summarizing a complex concept such as a business activity. Every business process or activity must somehow act upon, add value to, or change some subject. The verb-subject naming pattern makes this action explicit.

Any activity name that is limited to a verb can be improved by converting it to a verb-subject pattern. For example, in the television and radio business, an activity named, "Pre-emption" might be better named, "Pre-empt Programming." Very general verbs such as "manage" and "process" should also be avoided altogether. They imply no specific outcome. A name that is limited to only a noun can also be improved. In the IT services business, an activity named, "Help Desk" might be better named, "Deliver Help-desk Services."

A high-quality business activity (or process) name has the following characteristics:

The activity's name implies its outcome. The activity name should also imply the activity's outcome. For example, the activity name, "Process Account" follows the verb-subject pattern, but does not imply the outcome of the process. What changes once an account has been "processed" is not clear to the reader. On the other hand, the name, "Debit Account" implies that once the activity is completed, an account has been debited. With "Debit Account", the expected outcome of the process is implied in the name.

The name is already in use and recognizable to people in the business. To name activities in the model by the names already used by the business seems like a no-brainer. But, if the analyst is not familiar enough with existing operations and terminology, then he or she may need to elicit these names. Good sources, apart from speaking with employees in interviews and workshops, are existing business policies, procedure manuals, and training manuals.

Qualifier, if needed. A simple verb-subject activity name is ideal. But one or more qualifiers of the verb and/or subject may also be needed to adequately distinguish a business activity. The verb-subject name pattern with a qualifier can still provide a brief activity name, but even more meaningful one. For example, "Report Users" may be too generic a name, because there may be different activities that report users but differ in ways that are important to a particular process model. So, a qualifier is needed to distinguish one Report Users activity from another. One activity named might be named, "Report New Users", another activity named, "Report All Users", and yet another activity named, "Report Expired Users".

Keep these criteria in mind when naming any business process or activity. If an activity name does not have these characteristics, it should probably be revised.

ACTIVITY DEFINITION

Compose each business activity definition using the four-part Universal Business Process Definition.

A well-composed activity definition is worth the effort. Producing and including a concise definition for every activity in a business process model has several benefits. The effort is simply due diligence that reduces ambiguity about each business activity. An activity definition is also a concise, shareable piece of documentation for the process model's current and future readers. Having activity definitions at hand will improve productivity when eliciting the model refinements and it will serve the model's readers, in future project phases or projects.

Any business activity is just another business process. It just happens to be used in the scope of another, larger business process. So, the contextual meaning of any candidate business activity can be elicited and defined in the same way as any business process, according to the Universal Process Definition

Any business activity is:

1. A collection of interrelated work tasks,

2. initiated in response to an event (or events),

3. that achieves a specific result,

4. for a customer of the activity.

Normalize any candidate business activity according to the four-part Universal Business Process Definition (the technique is detailed in its own, earlier chapter). Compose a few sentences using the four constituent answers.

Example

Find Reservation – The Find Reservation activity is initiated when a passenger arrives for check-in at a counter or kiosk. It includes looking up the reservation by either the passenger's name, or reservation code, or the credit card that was used to make the reservation. Its expected outcome is that the reservation, that the passenger has arrived at check-in for, has been found and its reservation-related data retrieved. The found reservation and data are consumed by the Identify Passenger, Assign Seating, Check Baggage, and Print Boarding Pass activities.

At the end of UPMP Step 3, the business process model will have its third component – an Activity Catalogue. The model's in-scope business activities that are illustrated within one or more of the basic or refined business process flows will also appear in the Activity Catalogue. The catalogue will contain the clearly-written definitions of all business activities named in the model. The business activities have now been unequivocally named and defined. From here, each business activity's related specifications, performance measurement attributes, and configuration management data can now be additionally elicited and added, model refinements (throughout UPMP Step 5).

Exercise 4 – Define Business Activities

Review the notes provided to elicit the definition of CACHE activities and document them using plain language.

Review again the notes that were provided in Exercise 3 as well as the list of candidate business activities below.

- Register Supplier User
- Create Request for Quotation (RFQ)
- Browse and View RFQs
- Create or Update Bid
- Submit Bid
- Accept Bid
- Award Bid
- Purge Expired Bids

Define any two of CACHE's business activities.

Use the Universal Business Activity Definition Elicitation Agenda. Document your answer using plain language.

Compare your results to the proposed solution at www.ProcessModelingAdvisor.com.

UPMP STEP 5 – REFINE BUSINESS PROCESS FLOW(S)

Select and make the business process flow(s) refinements (and only the refinements) needed to meet the model's mission.

By the time this fifth step of the UPMP is reached, a cohesive foundation of integrated model components will exist: a mission statement (UPMP Step 1), a scope diagram (Step 2), one or more basic business process flow diagrams (Step 3) , and an Activity Catalogue (Step 4). If these model components seem sufficient to meet the model's mission, then one can proceed to validate the business process model in UPMP Step 6.

If the model components produced to this point are not yet contextually complete enough to meet the model's mission, then the components that have been established to this point of the UPMP form the sound framework of contextual knowledge and model components onto which remaining model refinements can now be added. Now is the time to focus on the various types of refinements that will meet the business process model's mission.

The reasons for refinements at this point will vary from project to project and from model to model, dictated by each model's mission. Though it may be contextually concise and syntactically accurate in its current version, refinement of a business process flow diagram's content will typically be required for the following reasons:

Not enough detail. The existing model may be too general to meet the model's required degree of abstraction. To date, only limited content may have been elicited and modeled given time/cost constraints, or perhaps few sources or details (access to people, documentation, etc.) were available, or limited business knowledge or modeling capabilities (elicitation techniques, modeling notation, or tools) may have been applied. Depending on the required degree of abstraction, logical or even configuration details may need to be added.

Too many details. When the model's mission is to present a conceptual degree of abstraction, it may contain too many logical details that would confuse or be of no interest to its reader. Too many sources or details may have been collected (e.g., via workshops), or modeled as a means of clarifying understanding (e.g., via brainstorming).

Contextual or syntactical errors. These are inevitable, due to limited knowledge and experience of the modeler, key stakeholders, limitations of chosen elicitation techniques, and/or the modeling notation or tools.

Reviewer comments. These will come via model review and validation (UPMP Step 6). Review comments raised in UPMP Step 6 – Validate Business Process Model typically lead back to UPMP Step 5 to make refinements, thereby improving the model's quality and meeting the model's mission.

In any case, business process modeling is a journey of discovery. UPMP Step 5 is about the efficient and disciplined discovery of those business process model refinements and only those refinements needed to meet the model's mission.

The remaining time and effort can now be focused on efficiently eliciting and documenting specific refinements until the business process model contains the right content and the right syntactical rigor to meet its mission. The business analyst may also be returning to this step to make refinements that will resolve key stakeholders' review comments received in Step 6 – Validate Business Process Model.

Most business process flow diagram refinements will fall within one or another common type, so a business analyst can become proficient by recognizing and handling most required refinements using one or another consistent elicitation agenda and modeling pattern. The elicitation techniques and timing used to elicit refinements may be different from those used to establish the basic business process flow diagram(s) or other model components.

To efficiently use the time available and produce meaningful process model refinements, a business analyst should ask the right questions. Only a few focused questions typically need to be answered to elicit each of the common types of business process model refinement. The UPMP offers a clear elicitation agenda for each common type.

Though BPMN offers a rich palette of graphical objects that can illustrate nearly any conceptual, logical, or configuration process flow concept, only a subset of BPMN objects and common modeling patterns are usually all that is needed to illustrate most business process model refinements.

What you should learn about refining a business process model by reading this chapter:

- What the most common types of business process model refinements are.
- How to decide what business process model refinements to make.
- How to elicit common types of business process model refinements using concise agendas.
- How to illustrate common types of refinements using BPMN.

Common Types of Business Process Flow Refinements

Most business process model refinements fall into one of ten common types.

Most business process model refinements fall within one of a handful of common refinement types. A competent business analyst should be able to elicit and illustrate any process model refinement of the same type in a consistent and efficient way.

Common types of process flow diagram refinements are:

1) Decompose Business Activities – The current model may describe the right scope of activities, but some of its activities may need to be decomposed because they are too coarsely defined to satisfy the model's mission.

2) Summarize Business Activities – The current model may describe the right scope of activities, but some of its activities may need to be summarized because they are too detailed to satisfy the model's mission.

3) Specify Conditional Work - Business policies and decisions will create logical conditions, that require periodic, additional work to be performed, on the way to achieving a business process's expected outcome.

4) Specify Errors and Exceptions – The model may need to communicate details about expected errors and exceptions, the activities that the process will perform to handle them, and in case of an unresolvable error, how the process end without achieving its expected outcome.

5) Specify Delays – The model may need to communicate where in its flow the process will be caused to wait, and the timing and/or duration of the expected pause.

6) Specify Data Inputs and Outputs – The model may need to communicate what data is retrieved or stored by activities, to and from data stores, passed among activities, or between activities and external actors.

7) Specify Assigned Responsibilities – The answer to "Who does what?" might need to be answered by the model.

8) Specify Process-related Datasets and Specifications – Though a picture is worth a thousand words, there are limits to what can be graphically illustrated. A scope diagram or business process flow diagram may be refined to make specific references to process-related datasets and documentation that is important to the graphical model's reader.

9) Detail External Actor Interactions – The model may be refined to include details about how specific activities in the business process will participate in exchanges (give or get something) with the process's external actors.

10) Specify Event/Outcome-Oriented Business Process Flow – The model of a business process flow may be refined to illustrate how alternate flows of activities are possible using event-oriented flow.

Each of these common refinement types can be elicited using a reusable, familiar elicitation agenda and they can be illustrated using a familiar BPMN modeling pattern. Being able to elicit using a clear concise agenda and being familiar with a relevant modeling pattern for common refinement types will ultimately help improve your efficiency as well as the quality of the business process model.

How to Choose Business Process Flow Refinements

Make only the business process model refinements that meet the model's mission or resolve key stakeholders' review comments.

Make only the refinements needed to satisfy the model's mission. Using the mission as a guide can help justify deferring a proposed business model refinement.

Before pursuing a proposed refinement, check that it would contribute to meeting the mission statement's three main parameters:

1. Would this refinement suit the intended use of this model by this model's intended user(s)?
2. Would this refinement be consistent with this model's required degree of abstraction (conceptual, logical, configuration)?
3. Would this refinement match the required tense of this model?

If a proposed model refinement does not contribute to meeting the model's agreed mission, then it should be avoided or the model's mission should be re-evaluated.

EXAMPLE

Recall the mission of the Airport Check-in business process model:

"Produce a logical business process model of the future Airport Check-in process that will comply with the new no-fly registry and regulations. The model will be used by the airport operations manager to determine which Standard Operating Procedures (SOPs) will be redeveloped and to train airline agents on the check-in process."

Based on this mission, we can expect to pursue any of these types of logical refinements.

1. Decompose Business Activities
2. Summarise Business Activities
3. Specify Conditional Work
4. Interruptions and Errors
5. Specify Delays
6. Specify Data Inputs and Outputs
7. Specify Assigned Responsibilities
8. Specify Related Datasets and Documentation
9. Detail External Actor Interactions
10. Specify Event/Outcome Oriented Business Process Flow

If we are familiar with the elicitation agenda (what questions to ask) and the modeling pattern to use to illustrate each of these types, we will competently handle any forthcoming refinements.

The upcoming sections of this chapter provide an elicitation agenda, BPMN modeling pattern, and an example for each of these common types of business process model refinements.

How to Decompose Business Activities

Decompose business activities that are too coarsely defined to meet the model's mission.

Perhaps the most common type of business process model refinement is to decompose at least some of the activities into sub-activities so that their tasks and other logical details can be better defined.

During UPMP Step 3 – Define Basic Business Process Flow(s), the goal was to elicit and document the structure of a business process' initiating event(s), basic flow(s), and expected outcome(s). The resulting basic business process flow diagram(s) now serves as the framework for activity decomposition.

But its activities may only be defined at a conceptual or high-level. The activities appearing in the basic business process flow diagram may serve as placeholders with the intent to be revisited and decomposed later, and maybe even with different elicitation techniques and different stakeholders than those involved in establishing the basic business process flow. For example, a basic business process flow diagram's activities may have been coarsely defined via a workshop with the intent that further decomposition its activities would be elicited later via documentation review or observation.

Any business activity can be straightforwardly decomposed according to the Universal Business Process Definition. Each activity is itself perceived and defined as a business process, that just happens to be used in a larger business process.

- A collection of interrelated work tasks (or sub-activities),
- initiated in response to an event (or events),
- that achieves an expected outcome,
- for a customer of the process.

Universal Activity Decomposition Elicitation Agenda

Decompose business activities using the Universal Business Sub-Activity Elicitation Agenda.

Use the three-part Universal Activity Decomposition Elicitation Agenda to elicit what sub-activities comprise a coarse-grained activity.

Universal Activity Decomposition Elicitation Agenda Item 1:

What causes this activity to start?

Determine the initiating event of the coarse-grained activity that is being decomposed. This is what causes its flow of sub-activities to start. Its initiating event may already be documented in the Activity Catalogue. If it is not, or if what causes this activity to start is in question, then it should be elicited now, as part of this decomposition agenda. Its initiating event will usually be implied by the expected outcome of its predecessor in the existing business process flow diagram.

Universal Activity Decomposition Elicitation Agenda Item 2:

What is the expected outcome of this activity?

Elicit or confirm the expected outcome of the coarse-grained activity that is being decomposed. The expected outcome of the activity being decomposed should also already be documented for this activity in the Activity Catalogue. If it is not, or if the expected outcome of this activity is in question, then it should be elicited now as part of this decomposition agenda. Its expected outcome will usually be the initiating event of its successor activity in the existing business process flow diagram.

Universal Activity Decomposition Elicitation Agenda Item 3:

What tasks need to be performed to achieve the expected outcome of this activity?

The tasks that comprise the coarse-grained activity can be elicited by starting with its initiating event and asking, "What happens next?" Once answered, the question is repeated until the expected outcome of the coarse-grained activity is reached.

Since tasks are just activities themselves, that happen to be used in a larger process/activity, each task can be perceived according to the Universal Business Process Definition. Tasks that do not meet the test of the Universal definition should be re-examined or discarded:

1. Is it (the candidate task) a collection of work tasks?
2. Is it initiated in response to an event (or events)?
3. Does it achieve an expected outcome?
4. Does it have a customer? (In other words, does another activity or stakeholder rely on its expected outcome?)

How to Illustrate Activity Decomposition Using BPMN

Replace a decomposed activity in the process flow using BPMN tasks or a BPMN Sub-Process.

Two ways to illustrate functional decomposition in a business process flow diagram are by including the sub-activities as BPMN tasks in the existing process flow, or by illustrating the decomposed activity as a BPMN Sub-Process (aka Collapsed Sub-Process) and adding a new diagram to the model to contain the sub-process's activities:

EXAMPLE

In the following sequence flow diagram, the Check Baggage activity is too coarsely defined to meet the mission of the model.

Original model:

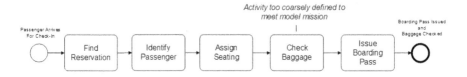

Through further elicitation, these sub-activities – *Weigh Baggage, Print Baggage Tags*, and *Attach Baggage Tags* – are found to comprise the task

Check Baggage.

Option 1: Add In-Flow BPMN Tasks – Replace the coarse-grained activity in the existing BPMN process flow diagram with the sub-activities that decompose it.

In the refined version of the Airport Check-in process flow diagram, the decomposed *Check Baggage* task is replaced by its three composite activities. More functional detail has been added to the existing Airport Check-in process flow diagram.

Refined model:

Option 2: Use a BPMN Sub-Process – Replace the coarse-grained business activity, with a BPMN Sub-Process (aka Collapsed Sub-Process). Illustrate that sub-process' activities in a like-named, separate process flow diagram. The level of functional decomposition that the Airport Check-in process flow diagram started with has been preserved, while some of its functional details have been added to the model in a separate diagram.

Original model:

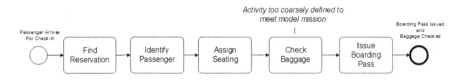

In the refined version of the original sequence flow diagram, the Check Baggage task is replaced with a sub-process in the model, and another process flow diagram is added to the model to illustrate the flow of business activities that comprise Check Baggage.

Refined model:

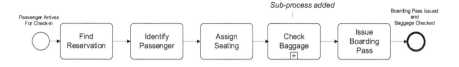

Plus, a new sequence flow diagram of the Check Baggage sub-process:

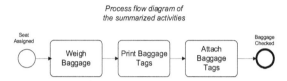

Remember: When new business activities (such as Weigh Baggage etc.) are added to the model, their names and normalized definitions should be added to the model's Activity Catalogue.

How to Summarize Business Activities

Summarize business activities that are too detailed to meet the model's mission.

Business activities may have been elicited and illustrated with too much functional detail to meet the mission of the model. Too much detail may be included in the current model for good reasons:

- to clarify or validate an understanding of a higher-level or summary activity,
- to encourage participants in the elicitation who may have described their activities at a detailed level,
- to understand or verify the scope of activities that comprise a major business activity, or
- because details were recorded during physical observations, detailed procedure documentation reviews, or staff interviews, just to name a few,
- an existing logical model is a basis for preparing a conceptual model of the same process.

But to meet the model's mission, it may be necessary to summarize detailed activities.

A set of detailed business activities can be summarized and replaced by a new summary activity in the model.

How to Elicit Summary Business Activities

Summarize business activities using the Universal Summary Activity Elicitation Agenda.

Any segment of detailed business activities in an existing business process flow segment can be logically bounded according to the initiating event of the first and the expected outcome of the last activity in the segment. These events bound all the activities that can now be contained in the new summary activity.

The initiating event of the first detailed activity in the segment becomes the initiating event of the summary activity. The expected outcome of the last detailed activity in the segment becomes the expected outcome of the summary activity. No scope or meaning is lost or added to the summary activity.

The new summary activity can be defined according to the Universal Business Process Definition and documented in the model's Activity Catalogue.

Universal Summary Activity Elicitation Agenda

Use a three-step agenda to elicit a functional summary of detailed business activities in a business process flow:

Universal Summary Activity Elicitation Agenda Item 1:

What is the initiating event of the first activity in the sequence flow to be summarized?

Identify the initiating event of the first fine-grained activity in the sequence flow segment being summarized. This is the initiating event of the new candidate summary activity.

Universal Summary Activity Elicitation Agenda Item 2:

What are the activities in the sequence flow to be summarized?

Step through and identify the activities and activity dependencies, between the first and the last detailed activities being summarized. These are the set of activities that comprise the new candidate summary activity.

Universal Summary Activity Elicitation Agenda Item 3:

What is the expected outcome of the last activity in the sequence flow to be summarized?

Identify the expected outcome of the last fine-grained activity in the sequence flow segment being summarized. This is the expected outcome of the new candidate summary activity.

Remember to name and normalize the new summary business activity according to the Universal Business Process Definition. Candidates that cannot meet the test of the definition should be re-evaluated:

1. Is it a collection of interrelated work tasks (What are they?),

2. Is it initiated in response to an event (What is it?),

3. Does it achieve an expected outcome (What is it?),

4. For a customer of the process (Who or what is it?).

How to Illustrate Summarized Activities Using BPMN

Illustrate summary business activities using a BPMN Sub-process and a like-named BPMN sequence flow diagram.

Use a BPMN Sub-process (aka Collapsed Sub-process) object to replace a summarized set of business activities in the business process flow diagram. Move the detailed segment of business activities into another process flow diagram, that has the same name as the sub-process.

BPMN Sub-process– Used to illustrate a business activity whose flow of sub-activities is described in another process flow diagram within the business process model. Whenever an activity appears as a BPMN Sub-process in a process flow diagram, the reader expects that the activity details are hidden in the current model, but it is detailed (functionally decomposed) in a like-named process flow diagram elsewhere in the model.

EXAMPLE

Assume you have established a basic business process flow diagram of the Airport Check-in business process.

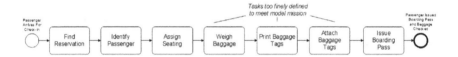

In reviewing this model, it may be decided that there is too much detail about the baggage handling activity to suit the model's intended use. It may be necessary to summarize these activities.

We will summarize the segment of baggage handling details within a BPMN sub-process named Check Baggage. Part of the existing Airport Check-in business process flow diagram is summarized. The refined diagram still communicates what causes the Airport Check-in business process to begin, its scope of business activities, incremental outcomes, and the same expected business outcome as before. The summarized model is still as contextually and syntactically complete as it was before summarization. *Refined model:*

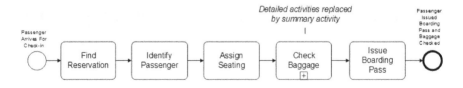

The detailed activities that comprise Check Baggage are retained in the Activity Catalogue and illustrated in a new, business process flow diagram called Check Baggage.

A new like-named sequence flow diagram detailing the Check Baggage sub-process:

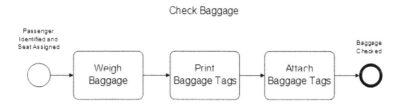

The new Check Baggage sub-process stands on its own as a business process. Check Baggage is a group of business activities, initiated by a business event that achieves an expected outcome that will be consumed by a customer (Issue Boarding Pass activity). The Check Baggage business process flow diagram illustrates these elements. It is syntactically and contextually complete. No contextual information about the Airport Check-in process has been lost through summarization.

Remember to update the Activity Catalogue to include the newly added summary business activity, Check Baggage, and its normalized definition.

How to Specify Conditional Work

Specify the policy/rule-based and decision-based conditions and conditional work to be performed on the way to achieving a process's expected outcome, to the extent needed to meet the model's mission.

The game of baseball is governed by rules that dictate what happens next, on the way to completing the game. For example, rules dictate that it's three strikes and you're out. In another example, its rules dictate that if a batter is struck by a pitch, that batter advances to first base, without even swinging at another pitch.

Business operations are also governed by policies and rules that dictate what will happen next under certain policy-based or rule-based conditions, while a process is being performed.

According to the Universal Process Modeling Procedure (UPMP), the sound contextual meaning and structure of a business process's initiating event, and expected sequence of activities, that lead to the process's expected outcome, have been already elicited and established. UPMP Step 3 has set the stage for the business analyst to elicit and add any conditional work to that contextually sound, unconditional structure.

Eliciting both rule based and decision-based conditions and work will focus on a process's already-established expected sequence of activities, that lead to the process's already-expected outcome. Its agenda is to determine: a) what business policies or rules will dictate and b) what decisions may cause additional or alternate activity to be performed, on way to achieving the process' expected outcome.

BPMN intermediate event objects will illustrate the business rule-driven conditions. BPMN Gateways will illustrate and business decision-driven, conditions, followed by activities to do the rule-driven, conditional work.

How to Elicit Specify Rule-Driven, and Decision-driven Work

Elicit conditional (Rule-Driven, and Decision-driven) work that will need to be performed on the way to achieving the process' expected outcome, using the Universal Conditional Work Elicitation Agenda.

The Universal Conditional Work Elicitation Agenda is focused on identifying whether what happens next (the work) in a process flow is unconditional, and if not, what is the business rule that dictates, or the decision that determines what happens next, and what the conditional activity will be.

Universal Conditional Work Elicitation Agenda

When using the UPMP, a process' expected sequence of activities have been established within a basic business process flow diagram in UPMP Step 3. The definition of each business activity was established in UPMP Step 4. These two contextually clear process model elements are the foundation, or baseline for clear and concise elicitation of conditional work.

If the basic or otherwise already-modeled sequence of activities that lead to the process' expected outcome is not unconditional, then the relevant business rules or decisions will be abstracted as either intermediate events or decision logic. In each conditional circumstance, the existing process flow diagram will be updated to include the conditional workflow that is illustrated by either by either a BPMN Intermediate Rule Event or a BPMN Gateway.

The Universal Conditional Work Elicitation Agenda asks, after the end of each business activity and before the start of the next:

Universal Conditional Work Elicitation Agenda

1) Is what happens next in the business process flow unconditional? If not, what business rule dictates, or business decision needs to be made, about what happens next?

2) What is the conditional, work activity?

EXAMPLE

The Airport Check-in process includes a Check-Baggage sub-process, whose initiating event, expected sequence of activities, and expected outcome are as follows:

Check Baggage

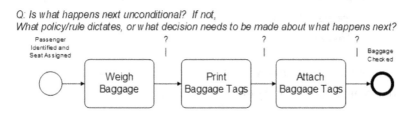

In the basic Check Baggage sub-process flow, the Weigh Baggage activity is unconditionally followed by Print Baggage Tags and Attach Baggage Tags. Once those activities have been completed, the Check Baggage sub-process will have reached its expected outcome: Baggage Checked.

Is what happens next after each activity in the Check Baggage process flow unconditional? If not unconditional, what rule/policy dictates, or decision needs to be made about, what happens next?

Elicitation Notes:

Q: Is what happens next in after Weigh Baggage unconditional? If not, what business rule dictates or decision needs to be made about what happens next?

A: No, it's not unconditional. The airline has a checked baggage allowance policy governing overweight checked baggage. That policy dictates that when a checked bag is overweight, we will not proceed to printing and attaching the baggage tags, until we resolve the overweight checked baggage.

Q: What is the conditional, value adding work activity?

To resolve overweight checked baggage, we'll give the passenger the option to pay an additional fee or repack their bags, so that each piece of checked baggage meets the checked baggage allowed by the airline's policy.

Q: Is what happens next after Print Baggage Tags unconditional?

A: Yes. The baggage tags must be attached to the bags for which they are indented, immediately after they are printed.

Q: Is what happens next in after Weigh Baggage unconditional? If not, what business rule dictates or decision needs to be made about what happens next?

A: No, what happens next is not unconditional. The airport's baggage handling policy dictates that if a checked bag is heavy enough to exceed the policy's heavy baggage handling threshold, it must have an extra, "heavy" baggage tag.

Q: What is the conditional, value adding work activity?

A: Attach a "Heavy" tag to a heavy checked bag.

We have elicited that that there are two policies that dictate when more work will be required, while performing the Check Baggage process (within the larger Airport Check-in process).

Policy or Rule	Conditional Work
Airline's Checked Baggage Policy	Resolve Overweight Checked Bag.
Airport's Baggage Handling Policy	Attach Heavy Bag Tag.

How to Illustrate Conditional Work Using a BPMN Rule

Illustrate conditional work using a BPMN Intermediate Rule (aka Conditional) Event object, or BPMN (Decision) Gateway, followed by the conditional, value-adding work, as a BMPN Activity.

BPMN Intermediate Rule Event – Illustrates a point in a process flow where a policy or rule conditionally dictates what happens next. It is an intermediate event, placed on the boundary of the activity to which the rule applies, and followed by the conditional activity.

EXAMPLE

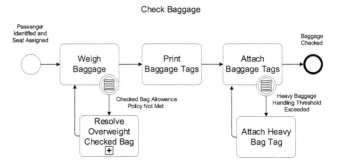

The diagram above illustrates, where the Check Baggage process will be supplemented by Conditional Work activities. Two business rules, will trigger the additional work to be performed, adding value towards the Check Baggage activity's expected outcome: Baggage Checked.

How to Illustrate Decisions Using a BPMN Gateway

Illustrate business process decisions made in a business process flow using the best-suited BPMN Gateway.

Use a BPMN Gateway object to illustrate business decision logic (i.e., logical If-Then-Else statement) in a business process flow diagram. The decision, illustrated as a BPMN Gateway, replaces the unconditional flow between the end of one activity and the next in the existing business process flow diagram.

BPMN offers a selection of specialized gateway objects to choose from, to depict the different ways that the decision is made.

BPMN Data-based OR Gateway – Illustrates a point in a process flow where a decision about what happens next is decided by evaluating a data value. Use the BPMN Data-based gateway to illustrate any data-based OR conditions in the business process flow diagram.

BPMN Event-based OR Gateway – Illustrates a point in the process flow where a decision is needed about what happens next is decided by evaluating an event. Use the BPMN Event-based Gateway to illustrate any event-based OR conditions in the business process flow diagram.

BPMN Complex OR Gateway – Illustrates a point in the process flow where a decision is needed about what happens next and is decided by evaluating a set of conditions. Use a BPMN Complex OR Gateway to illustrate any complex OR conditions in the business process flow diagram.

Tip: Use a BPMN gateway object that is best suited to the model's mission, specifically the model's intended use and required degree of abstraction.

Generally, use the BPMN Data-based OR Gateway whenever the model's mission calls for a conceptual or logical business process model. Only when the model's required degree of abstraction and intend use call for a configuration view, like in software development or low-code environment, would the differences in meaning between BPMN decision gateway sub-types become important to the model's reader.

Using a BPMN Data-Based OR Decision Gateway

Illustrate business process decision logic using a BPMN Data-based OR gateway.

Illustrate exclusive OR decision logic that relies on data values using the BPMN Data-based OR gateway.

EXAMPLE

The need to perform the conditional work to resolve an overweight checked bag was determined by the airline's checked baggage allowance policy (a rule). However, while performing the Resolve Overweight Checked Bag activity, the passenger will be presented with options, and then will make a decision about what happens next: pay a fee, or repack. It's a good practice to abstract this decision logic into an If-Then-Else statement: before illustrating it as a BPMN Gateway.

> *If* Passenger decides to Pay a Fee,

>> *Then* Pay Additional Check-in Fee,

>> *Else* Repack Bag

> *End if.*

Resolve Overweight Checked Bag

Using a BPMN Event-Based OR Gateway

When the required degree of abstraction is logical or configuration, and the decision is based on an event type, use a BPMN Event-based OR gateway..

Use the BPMN Event-based OR gateway to illustrate an event-based Exclusive OR condition in a logical or configuration business process flow diagram.

EXAMPLE

There are different ways that the Passenger Check-in process can be initiated when using an airport kiosk. This kiosk technology enables a passenger reservation to be identified using a reservation number, or the credit card used to make the reservation or the passenger's passport number. Entering a reservation number on the screen's keypad, swiping the credit card, or scanning a passport are all different physical events involving different kiosk devices. What physically happens next in the kiosk depends on the type of event that received the passenger's data.

This technology-enabled, decision can be abstracted into an If-Then-Else statement.

> **If**   Keypad Activated
>
> **Then**   Find Reservation by Reservation Code
>
> **Else**
>
> **If**   Passport Reader Activated
>
> > **Then**   Find Reservation by Passport ID
> >
> > **Else**
> >
> > > **If**   Credit Card Reader Activated
> > >
> > > > **Then**   Find Reservation by Payment Card
> > >
> > > **End if**
> >
> > **End if**
>
> **End if**

In this example, the decision about what happens next is made as soon as the initiating event happens. This can be logically illustrated using a BPMN Event-based OR Gateway, as follows:

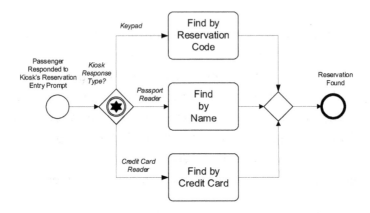

How to Specify Errors and Interruptions

Elicit and illustrate periodic process errors and interruptions, and what activities will need to be performed to handle them, to the extent needed to meet the model's mission.

The game of baseball is fraught with exceptions. Once the game starts, miscellaneous interruptions to the basic, normal flow of the game of the game and cause tangent activities to be performed. For example, the home plate umpire may call a time out, interrupting the game, to brush off the home plate, before resuming play. In another instance, a batter may dispute a strike call made by the home plate umpire. When that happens, the umpire will interrupt the game play to consult either the third or first base umpires and verify or overturn the call, and then allow the game to resume. Should sufficient rain begin to fall, the umpire may interrupt the game until weather conditions abate. If weather does not improve, the umpire may end the game altogether.

Exceptions may also occur while a business process being performed. Depending on the model's intended use and its required degree of abstraction, it may be necessary to elicit and illustrate the anticipated exceptions, and how to handle them.

Exceptions include errors that cause supplemental, error-handling activity to be performed. Errors that are unresolvable by the error-handling activities will cause the process to come to an end, without achieving that process' expected outcome. Exceptions also include interruptions that cause supplemental tangent activities to be performed, before the process can proceed towards achieving its expected outcome.

In more detail:

- **Error** – An error is an event that could periodically occur, and cause the process to stop until the error is resolved by a conditional, error handling activity. An error handling activity will perform the additional work needed to resolve the error event. Once the error-handling activity has reached its expected outcome, to resolve the error, the process will continue from the point where the error occurred, towards achieving its expected outcome. If the error handling activity does not resolve the error, the error-handling activity will bring the process to an end and the process will not continue towards achieving its expected outcome. It will end at an alternate, process-ending outcome.

- **Interruption** – An interruption is an event that will cause the process flow to be interrupted to perform a tangent activity. Once the tangent activity is completed, the process will continue on its way, to the process's expected outcome, from the point in the process where the interruption occurred. An interruption is not expected to cause the process to come to an end.

Step 3 of the Universal Process Modeling Procedure has already established the initiating event, and expected sequence of activities, leading to a business process's expected outcome (basic business process flow). That has set the stage for the analyst to follow the Universal Exception Elicitation Agenda to elicit the anticipated, periodic errors and interruptions that could occur while the process is being performed, and how to handle them.

BPMN provides intermediate event objects to illustrate where errors and interruptions may occur in a process flow. An intermediate event starts a process flow to, and returns from an activity that handles that event.

How to Elicit Errors and Interruptions

Elicit and specify process errors and interruptions using the two-part Universal Exception Elicitation Agenda.

The basic business process flow diagram and other model components, created up to this point in the UPMP have set the stage. The process's initiating event, its expected sequence of business activities, that lead to its expected outcome were established in UPMP Step 3 – Define Basic Business Process Flow. With that contextual definition of "business as usual" already established, the modeler has the solid foundation on which to systematically elicit and model what exceptions may occur, and what the business process will do about them.

Use the Universal Exception Elicitation Agenda to discover what errors or interruptions may periodically occur, and what error handling or tangent activity the process will perform when they do occur.

Universal Exception Elicitation Agenda Item 1:

What could cause either an activity or the entire process not to reach its expected outcome during the execution of a) each activity, or b) the entire process?

This question is posed for each activity in the business process flow and the business process as a whole:

1a. Each activity. During the execution of each activity, what could cause that activity not to reach its expected outcome?

1b. The entire process. Throughout the execution of the entire process, what could cause the process not to reach its expected outcome?

Universal Exception Elicitation Agenda Item 2:

What extra activity will need to be performed to resolve the exception?

EXAMPLE

Let's revisit the Airport Check-in business process.

Reviewing the Airport Check-in basic business process flow diagram, what events could occur during the execution of each activity or the entire process to cause that activity or the whole Airport Check-in process to not reach its expected outcome? What supplemental activity will need to be performed to resolve the exception and enable the activity or process to continue towards achieving its expected outcome?

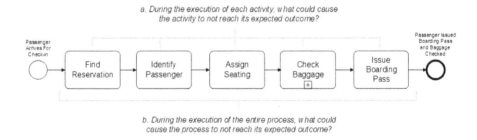

a. During the execution of each activity, what could cause the activity to not reach its expected outcome?

b. During the execution of the entire process, what could cause the process to not reach its expected outcome?

Elicitation Notes:

Universal Exception Elicitation Agenda Items 1a and 2:

1a - What could cause each activity not to reach its expected outcome?

2 - What extra activity or work will need to be performed to resolve the exception?

Q1a: What could cause the Find Reservation activity not to reach its expected outcome?

A: A passenger may have no reservation or an invalid reservation at the time of check-in. Here are a few common examples:

- A passenger may arrive at the airport to check in for the right flight but on the wrong day.

- Sometimes the flight is canceled; unaware of the cancellation, passengers arrive at the airport to check in.

- Often, passengers arrive too late to check in for the flight and it is not feasible to get through security, reach the gate, and get their checked baggage onto the flight in time for departure.

- Technical issues, such as converting the reservation system from old software to new software, could have caused reservation data to be lost in the conversion, resulting in lost passenger reservations.

If for any of these or other reasons, the passenger's reservation is invalid, then the rest of the Airport Check-in process (assign seating, check baggage and issue boarding pass activities) cannot proceed towards achieving the Airport Check-in's expected outcome.

Q2: What extra activity or work will need to be performed to resolve an invalid passenger reservation?

A: The passenger should be advised of why their flight reservation is invalid. They may try to rebook on the same flight or book another flight.

Conclusion: The invalid reservation exception should be handled by an exception handling activity – Resolve Reservation Not Found. If the resolve reservation activity cannot resolve this exception, then the passenger should be denied check-in, bringing the Airport Check-in for that passenger to an end.

Q1a: What could cause the Identify Passenger activity not to reach its expected outcome?

A: A passenger may arrive at the airport to check-in for a flight without valid identification. If the passenger cannot produce valid, acceptable identification, then Identify Passenger and the rest of the Airport Check-in process' activities (Assign Seating, Check Baggage and Issue Boarding Pass) cannot proceed towards achieving Airport Check-in's expected outcome.

Q2: What extra activity or work will need to be performed to resolve invalid passenger identification?

A: Invalid passenger identification can be resolved in a few ways. For example, the passenger should be advised of what identification is required and allowed to produce it. If they cannot produce any valid form of identification, then they should finally be advised that they are denied check-in. If the passenger is denied check-in, the Identify Passenger activity and the Airport Check in process for that passenger should end.

Conclusion: The invalid passenger identification exception could be handled by an error handling activity – Resolve Invalid Passenger Identification. If the Resolve Passenger Identification activity cannot resolve this exception, then the passenger should be denied check-in, bringing the Airport Check-in for that passenger to an end.

Q1a: What could cause the Assign Seating activity not to reach its expected outcome?

A: No seats may be available at the time the passenger arrives for Airport Check-in, because the flight may have been oversold. If there is no seat available to be assigned to the passenger, then the rest of the Airport Check-in process (Check Baggage and Issue Boarding pass activities) cannot proceed.

Q2: What extra activity or work needs to be performed to resolve no seats being available?

A: If no seats are available, there is still a way to resolve the issue. The passenger will be put on standby until the check-in period closes. If, when the check-in period closes, there is a seat available, then the standby passenger gets the seat assignment. If the passenger decides not to wait on standby, or when the check-in period closes there is no seat available, then the passenger is, given later flight options, booked on a later flight, issued a travel voucher, and their check-in process ends.

Conclusion: The no seats available exception should be handled by an exception handling activity – Resolve Seat Assignment. If the Resolve Seat Assignment activity cannot resolve this exception, then the passenger should be denied check-in, bringing the Airport Check-in process should come to an end for that passenger.

Q1a: **What could cause the Check Baggage activity not to reach its expected outcome?**

A: The Check Baggage activity could encounter several issues and there are several ways to resolve them. If a passenger has non-compliant baggage, such as too many pieces, oversized, or otherwise out-of-limits, baggage, then this can be resolved by paying extra fees, repacking, or special handling (e.g., oversized drop-off). If non-compliant baggage is not resolved, then the rest of the Airport Check-in process cannot proceed for that passenger.

Q2: **What should be done to resolve non-compliant baggage?**

A: A passenger with non-compliant baggage should be given options to resolve it by paying additional baggage fees and/or repacking, or even discarding baggage.

Conclusion: The non-compliant baggage exception should be handled by an exception handling activity – Resolve Non-Compliant Baggage. If the Resolve Non-compliant Baggage activity cannot resolve this exception, then the passenger should be denied check-in, bringing the Airport Check-in for that passenger to an end.

Q1a. **What could cause the Issue Boarding Pass activity not to reach its expected outcome?**

A: Nothing. Once the passenger has been identified, has a valid ticket, has a seat assigned, and their baggage has been checked, the issue of their boarding pass is a simple enough task.

Reviewing the basic business process flow diagram or otherwise refined business process flow diagram again, we ask part b of the Universal Exception Elicitation Agenda:

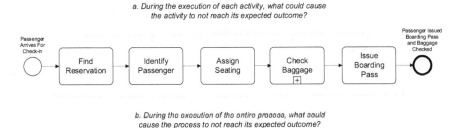

a. During the execution of each activity, what could cause the activity to not reach its expected outcome?

b. During the execution of the entire process, what could cause the process to not reach its expected outcome?

Universal Exception Elicitation Agenda Item

1b: What could cause the <u>entire</u> process not to reach its expected outcome?

2 - What extra activity or work will need to be performed to resolve the exception?

Q1b: What could cause the <u>entire</u> Airport Check-in activity not to reach its expected outcome?

A: At any time during the Airport Check-in, a passenger may have a complaint that is irreconcilable with what the airline check-in attendant has the authority to accomplish. For example, there are instances when a passenger is angry or uncooperative with the attendant. If at any time in the Airport Check-in process the passenger has a complaint that the check-in attendant cannot satisfy, then the rest of the Airport Check-in process cannot continue towards its expected outcome.

Q2: What should be done to resolve a passenger complaint during the Airport Check-in process?

A: A passenger complaint should cause the attendant to call for supervisor assistance. A supervisor has authority beyond the attendant's to perform activities to resolve any passenger complaints. The supervisor will use those to resolve the passenger's complaint and enable the Airport Check-in process to continue for that passenger. If a passenger's complaint is not resolvable, then the passenger is denied check-in, bringing the Airport Check-in for that passenger to an end.

We have elicited five exceptions that would require additional work to be performed so that the Airport Check-in process could continue towards meeting its expected outcome. We have also identified five candidate supplemental business activities that could be included in the model. The five candidate supplemental business activities can be normalized, defined and added to the model's Activity Catalogue.

Exception:	Supplemental Activity:
Reservation Not Found	Resolve Reservation Not Found
Invalid Passenger Identity	Resolve Invalid Passenger Identity
No Seats Available	Resolve Seat Assignment
Non-Compliant Baggage	Resolve Non-Compliant Baggage
Passenger Complaint	Supervisor Assistance

Neither passengers nor agents wish to run into these situations or have to do extra work to get through the Airport Check-in process. However, when such predictable exceptions do occur, we expect there to be a way to handle them so that we can get to the expected outcome of our personal Airport Check-in experience.

Using the Universal Exception Elicitation Agenda, we have discovered where exceptions could occur and what the process would do about them. We have also avoided changing the existing basic flow, or the initiating event, tasks, and customer of each of the activities that we have already modeled.

The existing business process flow diagram can now be refined to illustrate these business process exceptions, as well as what to do about them. The exception-handling activities can now be validated and included in the Activity Catalogue and illustrated in a refined business process flow diagram.

How to Illustrate Errors

An error exception differs from an interruption, because if an error is not resolved by an error-handling activity, then the process cannot continue onward towards achieving its expected outcome, and the error-handling activity brings the process to a controlled end.

Illustrate error exceptions using BPMN intermediate error event objects, and BPMN error end event objects.

BPMN Intermediate Error Event – Can be used to illustrate a business event where a pre-defined type of error is expected to occur.

BPMN Error End Event – Can be used to illustrate a business event that brings a business process to an end as a result of an unresolved error.

This is a useful error-handling pattern using BPMN. It does not change the basic or otherwise defined business process flow, or the expected outcome of the business process.

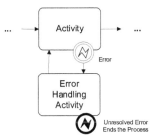

Error-handling Pattern Using BPMN

ERROR HANDLING PATTERN EXAMPLE

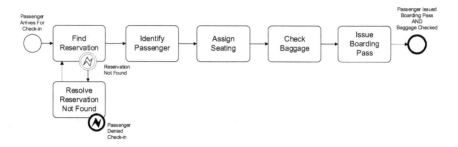

CASCADING ERROR HANDLING EXAMPLE

Here's a view of multiple possible Airport Check-in process error events. If any of the first-level error events (Reservation Not Found, Invalid Passenger Identity No Seat Available, Non-Compliant Baggage) cannot be resolved, then the passenger is denied check-in. If a passenger is denied check-in, then the Supervisor Assistance activity will start. If the Supervisor Assistance activity is unsuccessful in resolving the exception, then the Airport Check-in process ends for that passenger.

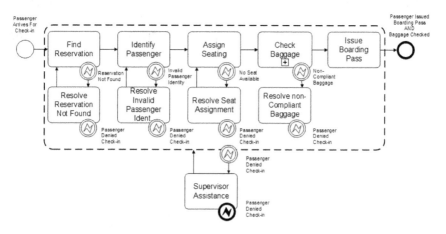

Using BPMN intermediate events, the exception events and the exception handling work needed to resolve them have been illustrated using simple event icons and alternate flow navigation, while the basic business process flow of the initiating event, expected sequence of activities, and expected outcome have been preserved and remain clear.

How to Illustrate Interruptions Using BPMN Intermediate Events

Illustrate process exceptions using the best-suited BPMN intermediate event object.

BPMN Intermediate event icons that can be used to illustrate interruptions include Message, and Multiple.

Event Type		Use
Message	✉	interruption caused by something arriving
Multiple	⬠	interruption caused by any one of several reasons

The following sub-sections demonstrate examples of how BPMN intermediate Message and Multiple event icons can be used to illustrate periodic interruptions to a business process.

BPMN Intermediate Message Event – Can be used to illustrate a normal exception event where a message has been received, while the business process or one of its activities is executing.

Let's consider the same digital arrival/departure board at the airport. The frequency of the signboard updates is controlled by the Broadcast Sign Board Updates activity of the Maintain Flight Operations Schedule process. While it's on, and whenever an operational notification arrives, the Display Arrivals and Departures process will receive the notification and update its display.

The diagram below illustrates that whenever a signboard update message arrives, the Display Arrivals and Departures process will perform its Receive Sign Board Update task.

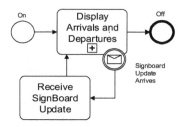

BPMN Intermediate Multiple Event – Can be used to illustrate a normal business event where any one of multiple predicted conditions has come true while a process is executing, causing the process to be interrupted and a supplemental activity to occur.

The diagram below illustrates that whenever an attendant needs assistance or a passenger requests a manager, the Airport Check-in process will be interrupted by the Supervisor Assistance activity. The Supervisor Assistant's initiating event and what happens have been added and illustrated, without reworking the level of detail or basic flow of the current model.

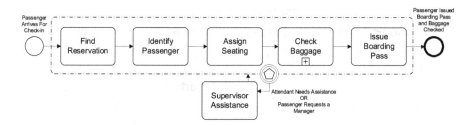

How to Specify Delays

Elicit and illustrate anticipated delays that may be encountered by the process on its way to reaching its expected outcome, to the extent needed to meet the model's mission.

BPMN Sequence Flow objects in a process flow diagram illustrate immediate finish-to-start dependencies among events, activities, and decisions. One might assume that activities will progress without delay, but in the real world, delays may be anticipated. Delays in process execution may happen because the process has to wait for people, systems, machinery, or information to become available. To meet the model's mission, it may be necessary to specify those anticipated process delays that may occur between the finish of any activity and its successor(s) in the process flow.

The established basic or otherwise refined process flow diagram is used along with the Universal Delay Elicitation Agenda to make the elicitation efficient and effective. The existing diagram provides the contextual foundation. The focus is now on the immediate flows between the activities in the business process flow diagram. The agenda will identify whether and why any delay would occur between the finish of one activity and the start of another, and what the impact of those delays may be on the process' execution. The elicited business process delays will then be illustrated using BPMN, refining the existing business process flow diagram(s).

How to Elicit Delays

Elicit business process delays using the Universal Delay Elicitation Agenda.

A delay is a pause that is expected to occur between the end of a business event or activity, and the start of its successor in the process flow. Once the delay has occurred, the business process will resume executing towards its expected outcome.

The purpose of the Universal Delay Elicitation Agenda is to discover delays that are predictable and are anticipated to occur at certain points or even throughout a business process' execution and will pause the business process on its way to achieving its expected outcome.

Universal Delay Elicitation Agenda:

Can each activity start as soon as its preceding activity in the business process flow finishes? If not, then when?

EXAMPLE

A project team developed a production deployment plan for a new enterprise application. The project team defined and documented a basic process flow diagram of the planned application deployment process. The model formed part of the installation plan and procedure. The project manager and her team created the model to develop a consensus about the identity and sequence of the planned installation activities. The project team used this model to concur on the key activities and dependencies. They also used it as their framework for developing detailed deployment procedures for each activity and clarifying assigned responsibilities in a deployment plan document.

The deployment process was planned to begin on Sunday at 8:00 am. It was also estimated that all the activities leading up to the start of the Enroll Remaining Production Users activity should be completed by noon on that same Sunday.

Using the basic business process flow that she previously established with the team and the Universal Delay Elicitation Agenda the project manager elicited contextually meaningful answers about deployment delays:

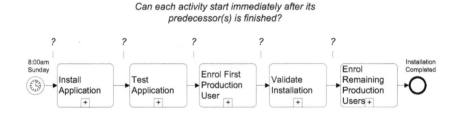

Q: Can Install Application start as soon as its predecessor is finished (at the 8:00 am Sunday start time)?

A: Yes.

Q: Can Test XYZ Application start as soon as its predecessor (Install Application) is finished?

A: Yes.

Q: Can Enroll Production User start as soon as its predecessor (Test Application) is finished?

A: Yes.

Q: Can Validate Installation start as soon as its predecessor (Enroll First Production User) is finished?

A: **No!** The person who will be the first production user will not work weekends. This activity will need to start on Monday at 8:00 am.

Q: Can Enroll Remaining Production Users start as soon as its predecessor (Validate Installation) is finished?

A: Yes.

By using the Universal Delay Elicitation Agenda, the project manager and team discovered an expected delay in their deployment process. The team discovered that the person responsible for performing the Validate Installation and Enroll Remaining Production Users activities would not be available to work until Monday. The delay would not change the sequence of activity execution or the expected outcome of this process, but there would be a delay in completing the process. Once the Test Application activity was completed, there would be an expected delay until Monday at 8:00 am when the process would resume moving towards its expected outcome.

The team also agreed that installation activities would be interrupted by a Team Briefing teleconference on Sunday at noon. Whatever activities would happen to be executing at that time would be interrupted, and the whole team would attend the Team Briefing call. The interrupted activities would resume when the Team Briefing finished.

How to Illustrate Delays using BPMN

Illustrate business process delays using a BPMN Intermediate Timer event flow object.

BPMN Intermediate Timer Event – Can be used to illustrate a time interval or point in time that occurs while a process is executing. The event marks a point in time at which the process will be delayed or interrupted and from which further processing will occur.

Example

Here is the refined Deploy Production Deployment process flow diagram. The process was still to begin over the weekend but would be delayed until Monday at 8:00 am when the Enroll First Production User would start and the process would continue towards reaching its expected outcome.

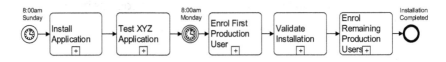

Here is the further refined Deploy Production Application business process flow diagram. At noon on Sunday, the process will be interrupted and supplemented by the Brief Team business activity.

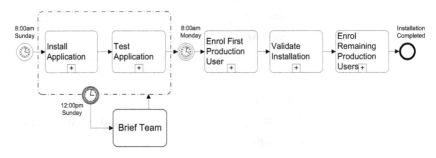

The elicited process delays were illustrated using BPMN intermediate timer events, added to the existing process flow diagram.

The refined process flow diagram illustrates:

- A BPMN timer event is used to illustrate the interruption to either of the first two activities on Sunday at noon. The group of activities that could be in-progress and interrupted at noon Sunday is illustrated using a BPMN grouping object.

- A BPMN timer event is also used to illustrate the delay in processing until Monday at 8:00 am.

How to Specify Data Inputs and Outputs

Specify the data inputs and outputs to the extent needed to meet the mission of the model.

Every process or activity uses some form of data input and produces some form of data output. A business process through the execution of its activities will receive and produce various data inputs and data outputs as the process progresses to achieving its expected outcome. Specifying inputs and outputs of a process or its activities can be important information needed to meet the business process model's mission.

For example, each of the activities of a payroll process that is initiated by a scheduled event (not an input) will consume data inputs and produce data outputs, on the way to achieving its expected outcome. It will consume inputs such as timesheet and employee benefits data, and produce outputs such as a payment file and journal entries, and other payroll outputs. These data inputs and outputs may be important enough to graphically communicate to the model's intended reader.

According to the Universal Business Process Definition, every process or activity has an initiating event and expected outcome. Its initiating event may be coincidental with the arrival of a key input. Its expected outcome might also be coincidental with the completion or sending of its primary output. However, this input and output may not be its only inputs or outputs. There may be others sent and received through the execution of a process or activity. Some processes or activities are not even initiated by inputs at all. They are initiated by events, such as schedules, business rules, or even simply their position within a defined process flow, but they still may consume inputs and produce outputs.

This elicitation focuses on what data inputs are consumed and outputs produced by each of the activities in a business process flow, between the process' initiating event and expected outcome. The Universal agenda for eliciting process inputs and outputs is simple and familiar: What data inputs does each activity in the process flow consume? What data outputs does each activity in the process flow produce?

The elicited process inputs and outputs can be graphically illustrated using BPMN Association, BPMN Data Object, and BPMN Data Store flow objects.

How to Elicit Data Inputs and Outputs

Elicit data inputs and outputs using the two-part Universal Data Input/Output Elicitation Agenda.

A process' inputs and outputs are elicited and defined by stepping through each of its activities and identifying what each activity will receive as inputs and/or produce as outputs.

Universal Data Inputs and Outputs Elicitation Agenda:

Use the two-part Universal Data Inputs and Outputs Elicitation Agenda to identify activity inputs and outputs.

Universal Data Inputs and Outputs Elicitation Agenda Item 1:

What inputs are received and/or outputs produced by each activity in the process flow?

Universal Data Inputs and Outputs Elicitation Agenda Item 2:

What is the source and what is the target of each input or output?

An activity may get an input from, or give its output to, another activity, a data store, or an external actor (process, organization, or system).

EXAMPLE

The basic flow of the Airport Check-in process is:

Elicitation Notes:

Q: What inputs are received or outputs produced by Find Reservation? What is the source and target of each?

A:

- Find Reservation sends a reservation search request to the reservation system.

Find Reservation receives a reservation search result back from the reservation system.

- Find Reservation passes the reservation ID to its successor in the flow – Identify Passenger.

Q: What inputs are received and/or outputs produced by the Identify Passenger activity? What is the source and target of each?

A:

- Identify Passenger receives a reservation ID from Find Reservation.
- Identify Passenger receives any acceptable personal identification (e.g., driver's license, credit card used to book the reservation, passport) from a passenger.
- Identify Passenger passes the accepted passenger identification to the next activity in the flow – Assign Seating.

Q: What inputs are received and/or outputs produced by Assign Seating?

What is the source and target of each?

A:

- Assign Seating receives a reservation ID from its predecessor in the flow – Idenitify Passenger.
- Assign Seating sends a seat assignment search request to the reservation system.
- Assign Seating receives a seat assignment search result back from the reservation system.
- If the passenger does not have an assigned seat or would like a seat reassignment, then Assign Seating sends a seat assignment update request to the reservation system, and Assign Seating receives a seat assignment update result back.
- Assign Seating passes the reservation ID to its successor in the flow – Check Baggage.

Q: What inputs are received or produced by Check Baggage? What is the source and target of each?

A:

- Check Baggage receives a reservation ID from the previous activity in the flow – Assign Seating.
- Check Baggage also receives a bag weight from a baggage scale.
- Check Baggage produces baggage tags to be attached to each checked bag.
- Check Baggage passes the reservation ID to its successor in the flow – Issue Boarding Pass.

Q: What inputs are received or produced by Issue Boarding Pass? What is the source and target of each?

A:

- Issue Boarding Pass receives a reservation ID from the previous activity in the flow – Check Baggage activity.

- Issue Boarding Pass sends a reservation search request to the reservation system and receives a reservation search request.
- Issue Boarding Pass also produces a boarding pass for the passenger.

How to Illustrate Data Inputs and Outputs Using BPMN

Illustrate data inputs and outputs using BPMN Data objects.

BPMN offers a variety of objects that can be used to illustrate process inputs and outputs:

BPMN Data – illustrates a dataset or a physical item that is an input or output of an activity.

BPMN Association – illustrates the flow of data between activities or between an activity and a database.

BPMN Data Store – depicts a source or destination of a data flow, where the data is being stored, such as a database or file.

BPMN Message Flow – illustrates the flow of data as a message between an activity and an external actor (system, organization, etc.).

BPMN Pool – illustrates the source or destination of data flow as a message between an activity and an external actor.

Process inputs and outputs can be illustrated in at least four ways using these BPMN objects:

1. Illustrate a dataset or a physical item as the input or output of an activity;
2. Illustrate the output of one activity passed as an input to the next activity in a sequence flow;
3. Illustrate data sent in a message between an activity and an external actor; and
4. Illustrate the flow of data between an activity and a database.

EXAMPLE

1) Illustrate a dataset or a physical item as an input or output of an activity, using a BPMN Data object

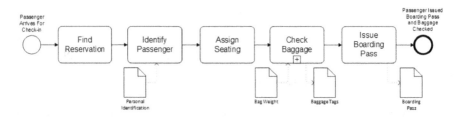

The diagram above uses BPMN Data and BPMN Association objects together to illustrate what dataset or physical item is passed into or out of activities in the Airport Check-in process flow:

- Identify Passenger receives any acceptable form of personal identification from a passenger.
- Check Baggage also receives a bag weight from a baggage scale.
- Check Baggage produces baggage tags to be attached to each checked bag.
- Issue Boarding Pass also produces a boarding pass for the passenger.

EXAMPLE

2) Illustrate the output of one activity passed as an input to the next activity in a sequence flow using a BPMN Data object.

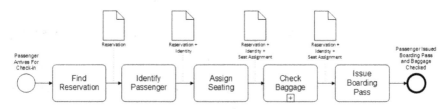

The diagram above uses BPMN Data, BPMN Association, and BPMN Sequence Flow objects together to illustrate what is passed from one activity to the next in the Airport Check-in process flow:

- Find Reservation passes the found reservation as output to the next activity in the process flow; Identify Passenger.
- Identify Passenger receives the found reservation as input from its

predecessor activity in the process flow; Find Reservation.

- Identify Passenger passes the reservation and identity as output to its successor in the process flow; Assign Seating.
- Assign Seating receives the reservation and identity as input from its predecessor in the process flow; Confirm Passenger Ticket.
- Assign Seating passes the reservation, identity, and seat assignment as output to its successor in the process flow; Check Baggage.
- Check Baggage receives the reservation, identity, and seat assignment as input from its predecessor in the process flow; Assign Seating.
- Check Baggage passes the reservation, identity, and seat assignment as output to its successor in the process flow; Issue Boarding Pass.
- Issue Boarding Pass receives the reservation, identity, and seat assignment as input from its predecessor in the process flow; Check Baggage.

EXAMPLE

3) **Illustrate data that is sent or received in a message between an activity and an external actor using a BPMN Message Flow.**

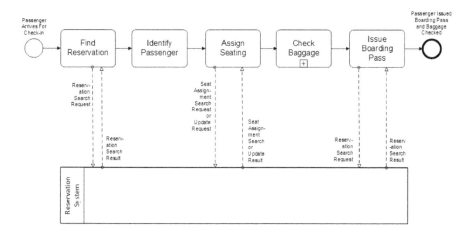

The diagram above uses the BPMN Message Flow and BPMN Pool objects to illustrate what data is passed from one activity to an external actor, the reservation system, in the Airport Check-in process flow:

- Confirm Passenger Ticket sends a reservation search request to the reservation system and receives a reservation search result back.
- Assign Seating sends a seat assignment search request to the reservation system and receives a seat assignment search result back.
- Assign Seating may send a seat assignment update request to the reservation system and receives a seat assignment update result back.
- Issue Boarding Pass sends a reservation search request to the reservation system and receives a reservation search result back.

EXAMPLE

4) Illustrate the flow of data between an activity and a database using a BPMN Data object.

Within the scope of the reservation system, it is the responsibility of the Answer Reservation Queries activity to receive reservation search requests, query the reservation database, and send reservation search results.

Answer Reservation Queries activity retrieves reservation data from the reservation database.

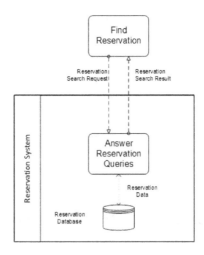

The diagram above uses BPMN Association, and BPMN Data Store objects together to illustrate that reservation data flows between the reservation system's Answer Reservation Queries activity and its database.

Example

Here's a consolidated view of the inputs and outputs that were elicited about the Airport Check-in process.

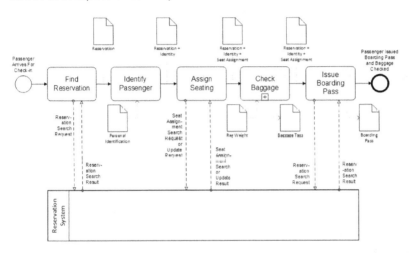

There are several ways to graphically illustrate process inputs and outputs using BPMN. When choosing which BPMN objects to use to illustrate process inputs and outputs, keep the model's intended use, reader, and required degree of abstraction in mind.

How to Specify Assigned Responsibilities

Elicit and illustrate assigned responsibilities for performing each of the process' activities to the extent needed to meet the model's mission.

One of the most common business process flow diagram uses is to specify who or what is responsible for performing each of the process' activities. Assigned responsibilities are typically illustrated using a swim lane diagram.

A swim lane diagram has its uses, but eliciting a process' activities using a swim lane diagram has a disadvantage. It is prone to a dual-purpose pitfall. Eliciting a process's activities and flow at the same time as assigned responsibilities can confuse the question of, "What has to happen?" with "Who does what?" This pitfall comes with risks.

- The business analyst and the modeling participants are prone to identify activities that lie within their responsibility (swim lane) but are beyond what is really needed to achieve a process' outcome.
- The activities that may be identified may be limited to the responsibilities that are familiar to the persons participating and therefore only represent a part of what's needed to meet the process's expected outcome.
- There may be a tendency for some modeling participants to equate the scope or number of assigned responsibilities with their value within an organization, and therefore identify activities that are above and beyond what is needed to achieve the process' expected outcome.

For these reasons, the UPMP avoids the dual-purpose pitfall of swim lane diagramming by first establishing basic business process flow in UPMP Step 3 and then eliciting assigned responsibilities as a refinement within UPMP Step 5.

While workshops or interviews are perhaps the most effective for eliciting assigned responsibilities, any of the common elicitation techniques such as observations, documentation reviews, and existing system reviews can be used. Involving the people who are or would be assigned the responsibilities will secure their buy-in. UPMP Step 3 and UPMP Step 5 can be accomplished in the same elicitation event, like a workshop, but eliciting and documenting the basic business process flow and establishing assigned responsibilities are two distinct agenda items.

The Universal Assigned Responsibilities Elicitation Agenda will simply focus on who is responsible for achieving the expected outcome of each activity in the process. The answer for each activity may be an organization, type of person, a software system, or sub-system. Answering this agenda may lead also to re-examination or discovery of new business activities in the existing business process model. For example, a responsibility hand-off from one role to another may indicate the need to break one activity into two.

Assigned responsibilities can be illustrated by overlaying BPMN swim lanes on top of a process flow diagram's existing activities. Each lane depicts a single role (organization, person, type of person, or system), and the business activities that are performed by the role simply appear in that role's swim lane.

How to Elicit Assigned Responsibilities

Elicit assigned responsibilities using the Universal Assigned Responsibilities Elicitation Agenda.

Simply asking the open-ended question, "Who does what?" is not really effective because it is prone to the pitfall of a swim lane diagram. If you ask a worker what activities they perform, that worker will identify activities that may or may not be important or contribute to reaching a process's expected outcome. If on the other hand, the basic business process flow's activities have already been defined, then identifying assigned responsibilities for those activities in that flow is a more focused, productive agenda.

Eliciting who is responsible for what is simplified when following the UPMP. The basic business process flow was established in UPMP Step 3 and the process' activities defined in UPMP Step 4. Eliciting assigned responsibilities is a refinement to an already established foundation of contextual knowledge about the process' initiating event(s), business activities, and expected outcome(s). The job of eliciting and modeling responsibility assignments is now less prone to being confused with eliciting the process' fundamental definition.

Use the Universal Assigned Responsibilities Elicitation Agenda to elicit assigned responsibilities. Step through each activity in the existing business process flow diagram specifically to answer this simple agenda.

Universal Assigned Responsibilities Elicitation Agenda:

Who or what is responsible for performing (achieving the expected outcome of) each activity in the business process?

EXAMPLE

Let's return to the Airport Check-in business process.

The Universal Assigned Responsibilities Elicitation Agenda is simply, **"Who or what is responsible for performing (achieving the expected outcome of) each activity in the business process?"** Since by this point in the UPMP we have established the expected outcome of each activity and at least a basic business process flow diagram, this agenda can be used along with the basic or otherwise refined business process flow to elicit assigned responsibilities for performing each of the business activities.

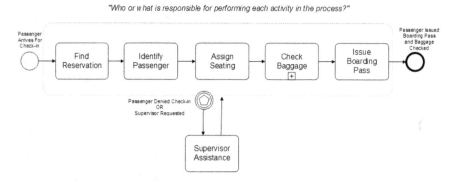

Q: Who or what is responsible for performing Find Reservation?

Elicitation Notes: The kiosk or the attendant consults the reservation system to determine whether the identified passenger holds a reservation. If there are several reservations held by a single passenger, the reservation with the next immediate departure will be selected and confirmed.

A: It is the responsibility of the check-in kiosk or the attendant to achieve the expected Find Reservation outcome.

Q: Who or what is responsible for performing Identify Passenger?

A: The passenger is a participant. However, it is the responsibility of the check-in kiosk or the attendant to perform (achieve the expected outcome of) the Identify Passenger activity.

Q: Who or what is responsible for performing Assign Seating?

A: Although the passenger is a participant, it is the responsibility of the check-in kiosk or the attendant to reach the expected Assign Seating outcome.

Q: Who or what is responsible for performing Check Baggage?

A: Although the passenger participates, it is the responsibility of the check-in kiosk or the attendant to achieve the expected Check Baggage outcome.

Q: Who or what is responsible for performing Issue Boarding Pass?

A: It is the responsibility of the check-in kiosk or the attendant to achieve the expected Issue Boarding Pass outcome.

Q: Who or what is responsible for performing Supervisor Assistance?

A: It is the responsibility of a supervisor to achieve the expected Supervisor Assistance outcome.

Q: Who or what performs Repack Baggage?

A: It is the responsibility of a passenger to achieve the expected Repack Baggage outcome.

This focused elicitation agenda has clarified which responsibilities are assigned to the attendant, the supervisor, and the passenger. In many airports, the passenger can choose to participate in the Confirm

Passenger Ticket, Assign Seating, Check Baggage, and Issue Boarding Pass activities by using a self-service kiosk or stepping up to an attendant's check-in counter. However, the answer to the assigned responsibility agenda question for those activities has been "The attendant or the kiosk".

INTRA-ACTIVITY RESPONSIBILITY HAND-OFFS
Responsibility hand-offs may indicate separate business activities, but not always.

The elicitation of assigned responsibilities may cause a re-examination of one or more business activities' definitions. According to UPMP Step 3, a responsibility hand-off is one type of activity indicator: "A shift in responsibility for work from one person or role to another indicates the end of one business activity and the start of another. When eliciting assigned responsibilities, it may be discovered that a responsibility hand-off occurs after the initiating event but before the expected outcome of (within) the same business activity, given the current definition of the activity in the model. This is an intra-activity responsibility hand-off.

The discovery of an intra-activity responsibility hand-off while eliciting assigned responsibilities begs the question of whether that single business activity in the current model should be broken into two business activities. The answer is dictated by the model's mission and is generally "yes".

If the model's mission justifies detailing assigned responsibilities, then decomposing one activity into two is justified wherever intra-activity responsibility hand-offs are discovered. If a responsibility hand-off is contextually meaningful, then the creation of two incremental activities, each with their own incremental outcome should be too. Remember, whenever an existing business activity is decomposed into two activities, then the model's Activity Catalogue and business process flow diagram(s) should be updated with definitions [i.e., initiating event and expected outcome] of the two new business activities.

How to Illustrate Assigned Responsibilities Using BPMN

Illustrate assigned responsibilities using a BPMN Pool and BPMN Lanes.

When using the UPMP, illustrating assigned responsibilities is a simple matter of allocating the activities in existing sequence flow diagram to one BPMN Lane or another. The "what" of at least a basic business process flow has already been established and illustrated in UPMP Step 3, so an existing business process flow diagram is the foundation on which to overlay the activities to BPMN Lanes and thereby illustrate assigned responsibilities.

The lanes within a pool illustrate which roles are assigned responsibilities for activities and where the assigned responsibility shifts from one role to the next. A BPMN lane itself does not change those other elements of the process. All other business process flow information, like events, activities, activity dependencies, and decisions remain intact when BPMN Lanes are graphically overlaid.

Using BPMN Pool and BPMN Lane objects to illustrate assigned responsibilities:

BPMN Pool – A BPMN Pool may be used to graphically illustrate the scope (boundary) of the business process, in the same way it is used to illustrate a business process boundary in a scope diagram.

BPMN Lane – A BPMN Lane may be used to graphically illustrate each of the roles assigned responsibilities for the activities that comprise the business process. Each BPMN Lane is embedded within a BPMN Pool.

The BPMN Pool represents the business process. Each BPMN lane within the pool illustrates a role that is assigned responsibility to achieve the expected outcome of one or more of the business process' activities. All the activities and decisions that are that role's responsibility are contained in that stakeholder's lane.

EXAMPLE

Here is the Airport Check-in business process flow diagram refined to illustrate the assigned responsibilities for the already-defined business activities.

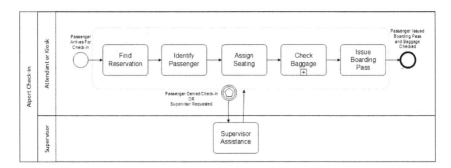

The model has been refined to illustrate the responsibility assigned to one role or another for performing each business activity without losing or adding the other contextual information about the business process.

How to Specify Related Datasets and Specifications

Specify the related datasets and specifications needed to meet the mission of the model.

A picture may be worth a thousand words, but the graphical components of a business process model may only fulfill a small part of a complete process specification. A complete process specification typically includes non-graphical text-based or data-based information about a process that can only be documented in non-graphical specifications.

Depending on an IT or BPM project's methodology, a business process diagram may simply serve as a roadmap for pinpointing in-depth related text and data-based process documentation. The events, activities, decisions, exceptions, etc. in the process flow diagram may be linked to non-graphical process performance data, procedural documentation, and technical specifications. Common types of process-related specifications are:

- **Process performance data**, such as volume, cycle time, defect, and cost data;
- **Procedural standard or template documentation**, such as business policies and standard operating procedures; and,
- **Technical design and testing specifications,** such as certain data requirements/models, software functional design specifications, and testing specifications.

Some examples of no-graphical process specifications are software use cases, test scripts, standard operating procedures, spreadsheets, and quality measurement data about a process that may be stored in spreadsheets and databases.

A business process flow diagram may, therefore, need to be refined to illustrate specific references among its certain process flow elements, like activities or message flows, to related non-graphical process specifications.

The agenda for eliciting business process-related data and specifications is simple enough: "What process-related datasets or specifications are relevant to each activity or flow in this business process?" Pose and answer this question for every activity and flow object in the process flow.

The answer might be the name of a software specification, operating procedure policy/regulation, or dataset of interest to the process model's intended reader. The unique mission of each business process model will guide the types and extent of business process-related data and specifications that should be of interest to the model's intended user(s).

Illustrating process-related datasets and specifications in a business process flow diagram using BPMN is graphically straightforward using BPMN Data or Database objects and BPMN association objects. A BPMN Data or a BPMN database object can be graphically associated with any business activity in the process flow diagram using the BPMN association object.

How to Elicit Business Process-Related Datasets and Specifications

Elicit related datasets and specifications using the Universal related data and specifications elicitation agenda.

Just like all the other types of process model refinements described in this chapter, the mission of the model and the basic business process flow establish a sound foundation on which to elicit process-related data and documentation.

This elicitation is also assisted by the established process model's mission and the established business process flow diagram.

Mission Statement – A BPM or IT project's methodology defines the types of process-related datasets or specifications that should be of importance. Process specifications or data that are produced in one project stage and consumed in subsequent stages may be important enough to be illustrated in the model for the model's intended readers in subsequent project stages.

Process Flow Diagram – The elicitation is focused on only those specifications and data sets that are associated with the objects in the established business process flow diagram, instead of on gathering and illustrating all documentation.

What business process-related data or specification artifacts exist or need to exist for each activity in this business process to meet the intended use of this model?

To elicit business process-related data and documentation one may step through each activity and simply ask:

Universal Related Datasets and Specifications Elicitation Agenda:

What process-related datasets or specifications are relevant to each activity or flow in this business process?

EXAMPLE

Let's consider the Airport Check-in business process,

The mission of this model (established in UPMP Step 1) is: *"Produce a logical business process model of the future Airport Check-in process to comply with the new no-fly registry and regulations. This model will be used by the airport operations manager to identify which standard operating procedures to write or change and to train airline agents in the new check-in process."* At least a basic business process flow diagram was established in UPMP Step 3.

With those important elicitation agendas completed and the resulting contextual knowledge established, the agenda to elicit business process-related datasets and specifications is now greatly simplified: **"What process-related datasets or specifications are relevant to each activity or flow in this business process?"**

Q: What process-related datasets or specifications are relevant to each activity in this business process flow: Identify Passenger, Confirm Passenger Ticket, Assign Seating, Check Baggage, and Issue Boarding Pass?

Elicitation Notes: We already have a standard operating procedure (SOP1081) covering the Airport Check-in procedures. It's going to need to be updated with whatever changes or new procedures come with the new no-fly registry. We also have a lot of data about the volume of Airport Check-ins at each airport. That check-in volume data is already being collected, and it is contained in the Monthly Flight Operations Report. There is also a TSA (Transportation Security Administration) regulation (reg. 821081) that we need to meet regarding checked baggage.

A: Given the mission of the model and these elicitation notes presented it becomes clear that the standard operating procedure SOP1081 and the TSA regulation 821081 are relevant specifications, though check-in volume data is currently not.

Through this focused elicitation agenda, relevant documentation was elicited about the Airport Check-in process. The business process has not changed, but the existing process flow diagram can be refined to illustrate to the model's reader the important, related text-based specifications.

How to Illustrate Process-Related Datasets and Specifications Using BPMN

Illustrate process-related datasets and specifications using BPMN Data, and BPMN Association flow objects.

Use a BPMN Data object to illustrate process-related datasets and specifications.

Use a BPMN Data object and a BPMN Association object can be used to graphically illustrate process dataset or text-based specifications related to one or more activities in the process flow diagram.

Each BPMN Data object can represent one dataset or specification. Any activity or group of activities may be graphically related to the same dataset or specification.

Before looking further at this example, this is also a good place to discuss the use of the BPMN Grouping object.

USING BPMN GROUPING

Graphically distinguish similarly affected scope of a process flow diagram, using a BPMN Grouping object.

A business process model may need to draw attention to a subset of the flow diagram that is affected by the same event, like an exception, delay, or error, or is similarly related to specifications. The BPMN Grouping object can be conveniently used for this purpose. Grouping does not itself affect business process flow, nor does it identify a process. It is simply used to segment or call out a subset of a process flow that is similarly affected by events or similarly related to specifications

There can be a few good reasons for grouping a subset of objects in a business process flow diagram:

- A group of business activities are all associated with the same documentation or annotation.
- A group of business activities are all affected by the same type of intermediate business event (like an interruption) in the same way.
- A group of business activities are all part of a scope of special interest to the model's intended user.

EXAMPLE

In the elicitation of process-related datasets and specifications, we discovered that one standard operating procedure and one dataset are related to the Airport Check-in business process. SOP1081 Airport Check-in Procedures specification includes procedures for activities: Confirm

Passenger Ticket, Assign Seating, and Issue Boarding Pass.

The SOP1081 Airport Check-in Procedures standard operating procedure is related to the whole process while TSA regulation 821081is related specifically to the Check Baggage activity.

Here is the refined Airport Check-in business process flow diagram refined to graphically illustrate the elicited related specifications.

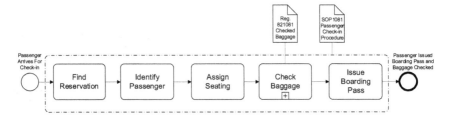

Use BPMN Data objects and link them via BPMN Association objects to the business activity or group of activities to graphically illustrate what datasets or specifications are related to them in the model. Each dataset is illustrated as a distinct data object and is related to one or more business activities.

How to Specify Event/Outcome Oriented Business Process Flow

Specify multiple alternate process flows using event/outcome-oriented business process flow.

Times have changed. Strictly procedural notions and flowcharting notations have become archaic. They were invented in the days of procedural language programming – in the last millennium. Those notions don't always work in today's business and technical environments. Today's distributed business structures, technologies like the Internet of Things (IoT) and cloud computing services have radically modernized the business process landscape. Today, a high-quality business process structure has been conceived, structured, and can be readily configured as a collaborating network of event-driven, outcome-oriented services, not just as a sequential procedure.

One characteristic of these network-enabled business processes is that they can have multiple alternate paths of execution. Depending on the mission of the process model, a sequential process flow diagram may not accurately enough describe all the alternate paths through a networked set of business activities.

The basic business process flow diagram established in UPMP Step 3 is an example of a sequential view of a business process. Activity dependencies are depicted as a sequential procedure, illustrated by sequence flows between the end of one activity and the start of the next. In this sequential view, the start of each business activity is triggered by the end of its immediate predecessor in the flow.

Let's examine the Airport Check-in process' basic business process flow diagram.

This sequential business process flow diagram is showing that the event named Passenger Arrives for Check-in is followed by the Find Reservation activity, which is followed by the Identify Passenger Ticket activity, and so on. A sequential view of a business process like this can be good enough when the business process' activities are always performed in the same sequential order, or when a conceptual view of the process is all that's needed to communicate the essential activities and dependencies. However, this sequential view may not be accurate enough to communicate with the model's intended reader, all the valid alternate paths of execution to reach the process' expected outcome. [In this example, the expected outcome is two-fold: Boarding Pass Issued and Baggage Checked.]

Does every passenger really proceed through all these steps, in this sequence in order to reach the expected outcome? No. Not all these activities need to be performed in this sequence for every passenger. What happens when a passenger arrives for check-in having already received a boarding pass using the online check-in process? What if the passenger arrives without a boarding pass and has no bag to check? Could the Airport Check-in process' activities be performed in an alternate sequence? Yes. There are multiple normal yet alternate paths through this process to get to the expected outcome.

If all of a process' activities need not be performed each time the process is executed, or if they may be performed in alternate sequences, then there are alternate paths through the process. Trying to resolve alternate flows by eliciting and illustrating all the alternate paths and the flow decision logic necessary to navigate among them using a sequential process flow diagram may become overly complicated. Some of the pitfalls of illustrating multiple alternate paths through a business process using such a sequential view are that it may:

- Take too much time and effort to elicit, illustrate, and validate all possible paths;
- Be prone to navigation logic errors as alternate paths are added;
- Become graphically complex as alternate flow navigation logic and flows are added;
- Impose constraints on when activities can start due to dependencies imposed by their position in a pre-defined flow (e.g. activity "C" may only start after its predecessor activities "A" and "B" are finished).

So, how can a process with several alternate normal paths be accurately modeled without overly complicating its process flow diagram? An event-oriented view of a business process flow can be an efficient and flexible remedy.

A typical business process flow diagram depicts the precedence or "flow" of business activities in a sequential view of the process that is graphically illustrated using BPMN Sequence Flow objects. The process' initiating event is followed by the first activity. The finish of the first activity is followed in sequence by the start of the next, and so on until the process' expected outcome is reached.

Using the Universal Business Process Definition and BPMN, it is also possible to understand and illustrate the same business process flow as a chain of activities' expected outcomes and initiating events. According to the Universal Business Process Definition, every activity has its own initiating event and expected outcome. The expected outcome of one activity may be the initiating event of the next, and so on. The activities of a business process can be perceived to "flow" according to incremental outcomes rather than according to their fixed positions in a predefined sequential procedure. The same sequential view of a process can be illustrated using an event-oriented view:

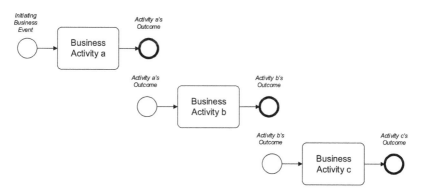

Eliciting and modeling a process using event-oriented business process flow, instead of a strictly sequential flow, can offer significant benefits.

- It enhances the modeler's understanding of the expected or "true" precedence or flow of the process' activities by clarifying its activities' incremental outcomes and initiating events, not just that the activities are performed.

- An event-oriented business process flow may have multiple logical alternate paths, and not all activities may need to be performed every time to achieve the process' expected outcome.
- It can discover where some activities may start as soon as possible, when prerequisite outcomes are achieved, instead of only by a set position in a sequential process flow.
- It avoids the elicitation and modeling of process navigation flow logic, reducing logical and graphical model complexity, making the model easier to read while reducing the risk of navigation logic errors.
- It will elicit a clearer definition of the true predecessors of each of the activities of a business process. It is not uncommon and it is contextually more accurate to discover that an activity's predecessor is not its position within a sequential procedure, but rather the achievement of one or more prerequisite outcomes. The prerequisite outcome(s) could be achieved by any one of several other activities in the same business process or even other business processes.

Because it illustrates events, BPMN can illustrate the precedence of business activities according to the activities' outcomes (end events) and initiating (start) events, rather than according to a sequential procedure. Because BPMN can be used illustrate an event-oriented view, it is also possible to illustrate alternate paths without cluttering the diagram with procedural navigation flow logic.

How to Elicit Event-Oriented Process Flow

Elicit event-oriented business process flow using the Universal event-oriented elicitation agenda.

Use the Universal Event-Oriented Business Process Flow Elicitation Agenda to examine each start-to-finish dependency in a business process flow diagram and to elicit event-oriented business process flow.

Universal Event-Oriented Process Flow Elicitation Agenda:

What outcome needs to be achieved before the start of each business activity in this business process?

The default answer is going to be that the outcome of each predecessor activity in the sequence flow diagram is needed before an activity can start. It may also be possible that the prerequisite that causes an activity to start may be achievable by more than one other activity, not just the one that precedes it in the purely sequential process flow diagram. There might even be a set of two or more prerequisite outcomes that need to be achieved before an activity can start, not only the expected outcome of its immediate predecessor in a purely sequential process flow.

EXAMPLE

Let's re-examine the established Airport Check-in basic business process flow diagram. It may conceptually describe the sequence of activities that most passengers will go through, but what if a given passenger has received a boarding pass before getting to the airport or has no bags to check? Are all the activities going to be performed and in this sequence?

We can elicit its event-oriented business process flow using the Universal event-oriented business process flow elicitation agenda. **"What expected outcome enables the start of each business activity in this business process?"**

Q: Universal Event-oriented Process Flow Elicitation Agenda:

What outcome needs to be achieved before the start of each business activity in this business process?

Q: What event enables the start of Identify Passenger?

A: Passenger Arrives For Check-in, the same event that starts the Airport Check-in process.

Q: What event enables the start of Confirm Passenger Ticket?

A: Passenger Identified (the expected outcome of the Identify Passenger activity).

Q: What event enables the start of Assign Seating?

A: The passenger needs to be identified (Passenger Identified) and have a ticket for the flight (Passenger Ticket Confirmed).

Q: What event enables the start of Check Baggage?

A: We need an identified passenger (Passenger Identified) and that passenger also has an assigned seat on the flight (Seat Assigned). Sometimes this activity does not need to be performed at the airport because the passenger has no bags to check.

Q: What event enables the start of Issue Boarding Pass?

A: We need an identified passenger who has an assigned seat on the flight.

(This iactivity is not always performed at the airport, because the passenger may have been assigned a seat and printed a boarding pass over the internet.)

Using this elicitation agenda we have discovered that expected outcomes of only some activities are necessary to enable the start of other business activities in the Airport Check-in business process. Certain Airport Check-in activities can be started by outcomes/events that might have been completed prior to arriving at the airport. Some activities may not need to be completed at all for certain passengers who have confirmed their reservation, selected a seat or printed a boarding pass online, or don't have baggage to check. In fact, if all of these outcomes have somehow already been achieved for a passenger, then that passenger may bypass the Airport Check-in process altogether and may proceed straight to security screening.

Activity:	Is Started by Event:

Find Reservation	Passenger Arrives for Check-in
Identify Passenger	Reservation Found
Assign Seating	Passenger Identified and Reservation Found
Issue Boarding Pass	Passenger Identified and Seat Assigned
Check Baggage	Passenger Identified and Seat Assigned and Bag to Check

Elicitation of event-oriented process flow will cause a re-examination of what causes certain activities to start. The initiating event of an activity is often the expected outcome of its predecessor in the sequential model, but not always. For example, a passenger who arrives at the airport having been assigned a seat before arriving need not perform the Assign Seating activity again. What causes Check Baggage to start is not its position in the sequence flow, but more accurately that the passenger has been identified and had a seat assigned.

How To Illustrate Event-oriented Business Process Flow Using BPMN

Illustrate event-oriented business process flow using BPMN Start and End Event flow objects instead of BPMN Sequence Flow objects.

An existing sequential business process flow diagram can be refined to illustrate the event-oriented business process flow by replacing certain sequence flow objects with event objects.

To illustrate event-oriented business process flow, the initiating event and expected outcome of each business activity become graphically explicit. A BPMN Start or Intermediate) Event object is used to illustrate the initiating event of each activity within the refined business process flow diagram. A BPMN End Event is used to graphically illustrate the expected outcomes of the activities.

The refined diagram will preserve the activities' dependencies as a chain or expected outcomes and initiating events.

EXAMPLE

Here (next page) is the refined Airport Check-in business process flow diagram that graphically illustrates the event-oriented flow for the already-defined process.

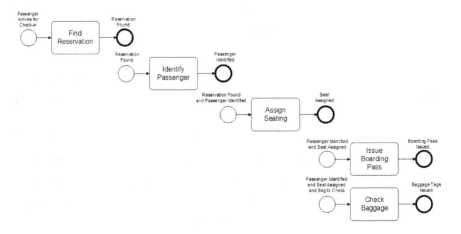

BENEFITS

In the event-oriented version of the Airport Check-in business process flow:

Basic Start-Finish dependencies have been preserved. A passenger may still arrive for check-in and progress through the process in the same sequence as described by the original diagram.

Activity sequence is more accurately modeled. Some activities of the Airport Check-in process are not always performed at the airport. A passenger may already have printed their boarding pass at home, so Confirm Passenger Ticket, Assign Seating, and Issue Boarding Pass are performed prior to arriving at the airport. A passenger may or may not have baggage to check, so that activity may not be performed at all.

Multiple alternate activities, paths, and timings through this process are

included in the model. The same model accurately depicts the sequence of activities that will take place for alternate scenarios, such as when a passenger arrives with boarding pass in-hand or has no bags to check.

Additional model complexity has been avoided. Illustration of control of the flow from one activity to the next is illustrated by events, avoiding the need to illustrate navigation decisions, and all alternate flow paths using sequence flows.

This process model illustrates where the Airport Check-in's activities could be logically integrated with other business processes, like the Online Check-in or Security Screening processes. Some of the same outcomes achieved in the Airport Check-in may also be achieved via other activities of other processes, like the Online Check-in Website process.

Exercise 5 – Refine business Process Flow(s)

Review the notes provided to elicit business process flow refinements and illustrate them using BPMN.

Here are notes from two different elicitation activities:

1. Meeting yesterday with Shaun O'Shea, Procurement manager:
2. E-mail received Ted Lee, Enterprise Security Services:

Notes from meeting yesterday with Shaun O'Shea, Procurement manager:

Chem AG procurement department will activate the CACHE user by:

- Verifying that the supplier exists in the SAP.
- Verifying the new user's identity with the named supplier.
- Activating the new user in CACHE (procurement staff will have CACHE userids, with the authority to do so).

- Once the new user has been activated, CACHE will send the activated user an email notification along with a temporary password.
- If the supplier does not exist in SAP then the procurement department will create a new supplier profile in SAP. If the new supplier does not qualify, then the supplier cannot be added to SAP and the process ends without reaching its expected outcome.
- If the supplier user's identity cannot be validated, then the supplier user ID cannot be activated in CACHE and the process ends without reaching its expected outcome.

E-mail received this morning from Ted Lee, Enterprise Security Services:

Good Day:

Thanks for your call this morning. As we discussed, you will have to integrate CACHE with our existing user management system.

To get a temporary password for a new CACHE user, the CACHE system will need to send the new user's userid (Temporary Password Request) to the enterprise user management system.

The user management system is a shared enterprise service that will receive the request, create a temporary password, create or update that userid's information in the database, and send the assigned temporary password (Temporary Password Response) for that userid back to CACHE.

Your developers will want to refer to the Chem AG Enterprise User Management specification for all the details on this and for technical details about all the other user management messaging and services, such as User Authentication, Change Password, Forgot Password, and Deactivate User.

Let me know if you have any questions.

Ted

Review the elicited refinements, and refine the business process flow diagram(s) and scope diagram as necessary.

a. Decompose the Activate Supplier User activity.

b. Specify the exceptions that could occur while activating a CACHE user and what to do about them.

c. Specify the external stakeholder interaction between CACHE and the enterprise user management system to obtain a temporary password. Illustrate documentation related to this part of the process. Illustrate where user management data is stored.

d. Specify the assigned responsibilities for Register CACHE Supplier User activities.

Compare your results to the proposed solution at www.ProcessModelingAdvisor.com.

UPMP Step 6 - Validate Business Process Model

Measure whether the business process model's quality is good enough.

Think of, in your experience, a business process model that was of poor quality. If it was not fit enough for its intended use, was it because of poor contextual quality, poor syntactical quality, or both? Did it fall short in its lack of business accuracy, key stakeholder participation, model configuration, or modeling syntax?

A high-quality process model is simply one that is fit enough for its intended use. It is contextually accurate enough. It describes real-world facts about the process accurately and at about the right degree of abstraction. It is also syntactically accurate enough. It contains the appropriate model components and types of refinements, using the format, notation, and language understood by its intended users.

Project scopes, objectives, methodologies, key stakeholders' expectations and constraints vary from one business process improvement or IT project to the next. With all of these variables at play, it may seem difficult to objectively quantify what a high-quality business process model should be. However, a high-quality model is achievable by following the defined UPMP approach, and its quality can be measured according to the Universal business process model quality factors.

Two practical approaches for achieving high quality are quality assurance and quality control. The UPMP applies both of these strategies.

Consistently following a defined process for producing products and practicing it from one project to the next is a quality assurance strategy. The UPMP is a defined process for producing business process models and it can be adopted, repeated, and refined from one project to the next to establish, practice, and improve one's business process modeling competence.

Conducting model work product reviews to identify errors and omissions is a quality control strategy. UPMP Step 6 is a quality control step. It can be used to assess a process model's quality according to the Universal business process model quality factors given in this chapter. Once this review step is completed a decision can be made about whether the model meets its intended use and modeling can end or, further refinement or rework needs to be performed.

Self-reviews, peer reviews and client reviews are common process model review techniques. The Universal Business Process Model Quality Checklists offered in this chapter provide the objective review criteria.

A business analyst can choose and tailor the timing, review techniques and select the criteria used to validate that project's business process model and still consistently assess that model's quality in a consistent way to other projects' models. UPMP Step 6 may be performed at the end of the model's development once all the components of the model have been produced, or as each of UPMP Steps 1 through 5 and the model's main components are completed.

Refining or reworking some aspects of the model resolves review comments that are generated by UPMP Step 6. If and once a process model is good enough to meet its intended use the entire modeling activity can come to an end.

What you should learn about validating a business process model's quality by reading this chapter:

- How business process model quality can be measured.
- What business process model review techniques to use.
- How to tailor the scope and timing of review activities.
- How to assess business process model quality using the Universal Business Process Model Quality Criteria.
- How to document business process model quality using checklists.

Universal Business Process Model Quality Factors

The quality of a business process model is measurable according to Universal Business Process Model Quality Factors.

A high-quality business process model is simply one that is fit enough for its intended use. Despite all the possible business process model uses, in various methodologies, and that fact that no two projects are the same, the Universal Business Process Model Quality Factors enables a structured and relevant way to assess business process model quality.

There are four underlying quality factors, that most significantly predict any business process model's fitness for use.

Universal Business Process Model Quality Factors

1. Fitness for Use			
1.1. Contextual Quality		1.2. Syntactical Quality	
1.1.1 Business Accuracy	1.1.2 Key Stakeholder Participation	1.1.3 Model Configuration	1.1.4 Modeling Notation

A process model's fitness for use is founded on its contextual and syntactical qualities.

Its contextual quality is the extent to which the model is accurate enough for its intended use by its intended user(s). A business process model's contextual quality is primarily driven by two contextual quality factors: business accuracy and key stakeholder participation.

A business process model's syntactical quality is the extent to which the model contains the model components and adheres well enough to its chosen language and notation for its intended use and reader. Its syntactical quality is primarily driven by two syntactical quality factors:

the model's configuration and its notation.

If these factors are sufficiently present in a business process model, that model's development can come to an end. If they are not sufficiently present, then some rework should be performed.

Universal Business Process Model Quality Factors underlie any business process model's quality:

1) **Fitness for Use** – Is the business process model fit enough to meet this model's mission?

   a. **Contextual Quality** – Is the business process model's contextual quality good enough to meet this model's mission?

      i. **Business Accuracy** – Is this business process model's degree of abstraction precise enough for its intended use?

      ii. **Key Stakeholder Participation** – Have this business process model's key stakeholders participated enough in its elicitation and review?

   b. **Syntactical Quality** – Is the model's syntactical quality good enough to meet this model's mission?

      i. **Model Configuration** – Does this business process model include those components and refinements (and only those components and refinements) for its intended use?

      ii. **Modeling Notation** – Does this model adhere well enough to its chosen syntax?

BUSINESS ACCURACY

The business accuracy quality factor is the extent to which the business process model is detailed enough or generalized enough for its intended use.

Any business process model is an abstraction of the real world. A high-quality business process model abstracts the real-world business operations to the degree that suits the model's intended use.

Three commonly understood degrees of abstraction for analysis models are conceptual, logical, and configuration. A conceptual business process model is sufficient for uses like scoping or sizing an IT or BPM project. But lacks details needed to measure existing processes, design operating procedures, or design software. For those uses, a logical degree of abstraction is likely needed. A configuration model is one that describes the configuration of a workflow within a software system, or named physical devices, software modules, operating procedures.

Following the UPMP, a process model's intended use and required degree of abstraction were established in UPMP Step 1, when defining the model's mission. In UPMP Step 6, you can objectively assess whether the competed model's degree of abstraction is consistent with its mission.

Is this business process model's degree of abstraction suitable for its intended use?

KEY STAKEHOLDER PARTICIPATION

The key stakeholder participation quality factor is the extent to which

the business process model's key stakeholders have participated in the model's development.

Key stakeholder participation is perhaps the most important quality factor. In practical terms, if the business analyst believes he has produced a very good model, but the project's key stakeholders are not convinced, then it is not a high-quality business process model.

On any given BPM or IT project, there may be as many perceptions of what a high-quality business process model should be as there are points of view, at least at the start of the analysis.

Therefore, a competent business analyst does not work in isolation, but rather facilitate key stakeholders' participation. There are a few types of key stakeholders to consider:

Project Owner(s) – A person who is funding the project.

Business Domain Expert(s) – A person who performs or will perform the business process.

Model Consumer(s) – A person who will consume the business process model as an input to their role on an IT or BPM project.

Special Interest Stakeholder(s) – A person who has a supporting role or influence in the model. For example, enterprise architects, auditors, or vendors who may not be the owners, business domain experts, or consumers of the model, but may have a supporting role and the power to influence the quality of the model.

The key stakeholder participation quality factor is the extent to which key stakeholders have been involved in the model's elicitation and validation. A model that has had key stakeholders' participation in its elicitation and review will reflect those participants' perceptions of what's going on in the business. It will be much more likely to meet their expectations than a model that they have not been consulted about.

The key stakeholder participation quality factor is measured in UPMP Step 6 by eliciting an answer to the question:

Have this business process model's key stakeholders participated enough in its elicitation and review?

MODEL CONFIGURATION

The model configuration quality factor is the extent to which the business process model includes the model components and refinement types needed to meet the model's mission.

A business process model is comprised of model components. The model components produced by UPMP Steps 1 through 5 are a mission statement, scope diagram, activity catalog, and basic business process flow diagram(s) and refined business process flow diagram(s) and may also refer to process-related data and specifications. However, the model's intended use, which will vary from one project to the next will determine what the "correct" model configuration - whether all these need to be included in the model - should be.

A conceptual scope diagram may be all that's required to describe a process and be an input into a feasibility, proposal, or planning phase of an IT project. On the other end of the spectrum, detailed process flow diagrams, along with process-related measurement data and specifications (like control data and control charts), might be required as input to a process management or improvement project.

In UPMP Step 1 the model's mission defines each business process model's intended use. Model configuration quality is assessed in UPMP Step 6 by eliciting an answer to the question:

Does this business process model include the model components and refinements and only the components and refinements needed to meet its intended use?

MODELING NOTATION

Modeling notation quality is the extent to which the model adheres to

a chosen language and modeling notation.

A high-quality business process model adheres to a chosen modeling notation well-enough to meet the model's intended use.

A common language is needed for effective communication. What has been elicited needs to be accurately-enough, communicated, and understood by the model's readers. While native language is used to document text-based information, there are many modeling notations available for process diagramming. These include functional decomposition, data flow, activity diagrams, and basic flowcharts.

BPMN is not only capable of illustrating strictly procedural process flows and logical details like swim lanes. It is differentiated from other notations by its ability to illustrate events and messages, essential to modern, event and outcome-oriented business process structures, and the technologies that implement them.

The model's mission should dictate the notation used and the rigor with which it is followed. For example, a BPMN collaboration diagram can be used to illustrate process scope to a technical audience who is familiar with and expects BPMN. On the other hand, any other notation might better hold the attention of a non-technical audience while communicating the scope of a business process. For example, if it would better hold the attention of a model's non-technical audience, business process scope might be illustrated using clip art flow objects or logos instead of BPMN pools. The same is true of process flow diagrams. If the model's intended audience will not gain anything from interpreting different BPMN event objects, then why not just use generic (BPMN None) event flow objects to illustrate business events?

A business process model's modeling notation quality can be measured by the extent that the model follows a chosen notation to suit its intended use and audience.

Modeling notation quality is measured in UPMP Step 6 by eliciting an answer to the question:

Does this model adhere well enough to its chosen syntax?

How to Elicit Business Process Model Quality

Elicit business process model quality using common elicitation techniques and the Universal Business Process Model Quality Criteria.

A business process model's quality can be objectively measured using common review techniques together with the Universal Business Process Model Quality Criteria. Reviews may be performed either incrementally as each model component is completed, or after the first five UPMP steps and the model have been completed. The Universal Business Model Quality Factors are stated as questions that can be used as the review agenda and answered with a yes or no. This agenda is organized according to the Universal business process model quality factors.

Review Techniques

Assess business process model quality using self-reviews, peer reviews, and/or client reviews.

Choose review techniques, timing or reviews, reviewers, and review agenda that best suit the time, cost, and other constraints of the project. The choice will be mostly influenced by the project's organization, the accessibility, availability, and knowledge of key stakeholders who may participate, as well as the project budget and schedule.

Three techniques that are well-suited for eliciting quality review comments are:

Self-Review– Review and revise the model before completing it.

Peer-Review – Review the model with peers among the project team and resolve review comments before distributing it.

Client Verification Review – Review the model with whoever will consume it and resolve review comments before finalizing it.

Reviews may be conducted whenever a significant model component is added or changed, namely at the end of each modeling step. A minimum of one review should be conducted before the process model is deemed finished.

The elicitation techniques applied to validate a business process model generally depend on who is involved in the review. Validation of a business process model relies on involving people in the reviews. There are two types of key stakeholders who should participate in process model reviews.

1. People whose work is described or affected by a process model have ownership, communicate ideas, and are in the best position to confirm or deny whether it describes the business correctly.
2. People who will consume a business process model are in the best position to validate its configuration and use of chosen syntax.

Regardless of the type of model review, the elicitation technique(s) employed, and the reviewers involved, the review agenda will be the same. For validation reviews to be most effective, the review agenda should be a founded on an agreed set of evaluation criteria that will test for the required quality factors. The agenda for validating a business process model's quality should focus on the same key quality factors, regardless of the review techniques and reviewers used. This means following an agenda of asking and answering questions that validate that the necessary quality factors are sufficiently present in the model.

If the review results indicate that the model does not yet meet its intended use, then the model will require some further refinement by reiterating one or more of the steps of the UPMP. The amount of effort spent to refine the model to resolve review comments will typically be constrained by project budget and schedule.

BUSINESS PROCESS MODEL QUALITY REVIEW TIPS

Tailor the scope and timing of validation activities to the unique project constraints and opportunities of each project.

Methodologies, organizational culture and standards, stakeholder participation, and other dynamics can vary widely from one project to the next. These dynamics justify or impose some tailoring of the quality review activities.

A good practice, especially when producing large or complex business process models, is to review model components incrementally, at least informally, against the Universal Business Process Model Quality factors as soon as each component is produced, at the end of each step, and before moving ahead to the next step. This way the business analyst is not working in isolation, and obvious omissions or changes can be identified and resolved before too much time is invested. The impact of review comments and resulting changes can be limited to model components that have been produced to date.

For simpler models, a business analyst may also elect to defer validating the business process model until that last step of the UPMP. For example, the analyst would perform Step 6 once developing and documenting business process model is complete. Whenever elicitation and modeling are finished, holding a validation workshop (using the process model quality presented in this book as the agenda) can achieve final acceptance and completion of the business process model.

Validating that a model meets agreed textual and graphical standards is probably the easiest quality factor to assess in a business process model. A business analyst and his peers typically have a strong enough command of their spoken and written language, to validate the textual components of a model through peer reviews of text-based model components. Their knowledge of the chosen graphical notation is normally sufficient enough to validate the quality of the model's graphical components. In the case of BPMN, there is a published standard, and there are several references in books and on the internet to draw from about the BPMN notation. If process modeling software is being used to illustrate the model, the software may have features to enforce the notation's rules. In addition to such tools, a large organization may also have some format or style standards to be followed.

How to Document Business Process Model Quality

Document business process model quality using the Universal Business Process Model Quality Checklists.

A checklist is a practical way to communicate a consistent and objective review agenda (criteria) and to document the review results and comments. It clearly and concisely communicates the same review criteria to both a process modeler and a model's reviewer(s). It informs the modeler about the specific quality criteria that should be met. It enables a model's reviewer(s) to be relatively consistent and objective. A completed checklist is easy to share and provides evidence of completed review activities.

Use the Universal Business Process Model Quality Checklists to communicate the quality factors and document the review results for any business process model. Its review criteria are stated simply so that reviewers should be able to provide a simple yes/no answer to each criterium. It's organized into five component checklists.

The modeler can choose to use only the top-level Universal Process Model Fitness For Use Quality Checklist or to dive deeper by including any or all of the four underlying checklists: Business Accuracy, Key Stakeholder Participation, Model Configuration, and Modeling Syntax. If a simple or summary review is all that's needed, then the first level Fitness for Use Checklist will suffice. If a more detailed or factor-specific review is desired, then one or more of the detailed checklists can also be included to form the review agenda.

Universal
Process Model Quality Checklists

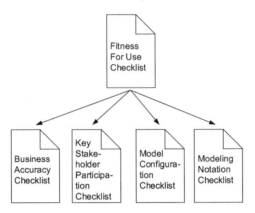

The quality factors that comprise each of the five checklists are detailed in Appendix 2 – Universal Business Process Model Quality Checklist.

UNIVERSAL BUSINESS PROCESS MODEL QUALITY CHECKLIST EXAMPLE

A customizable spreadsheet version of the Universal Business Process Model Quality Checklists is available at www.ProcessModelingAdvisor.com.

Quality Ffactor	Assessment Leve	Criteria	Criteria Met? Y/N	Comment/Reason
Fitness For Use	1	Is this model good enough for its intended use?		
Fitness For Use	2	Is this model's contextual quality good enough for its intended use?		
Business Accuracy	3	Is this model's business accuracy good enough for its intended use?		
Key Stakeholder Participation	3	Is this model's key stakeholder participation quality good enough for its intended use?		
Fitness For Use	2	Is this model's syntactical quality good enough for its intended use?		
Model Configuration	3	Is this model's configuration quality good enough for its intended use?		
Modeling Notation	3	Is this model's notation quality good enough for its intended use?		
Business Accuracy	4	Is the model's mission statement accurate?		
Business Accuracy	5	Is the model's required tense (current or future) defined and accurate?		
Business Accuracy	5	Is the model's required degree of abstraction (conceptual, logical, or physical) defined and accurate?		
Business Accuracy	5	Are model's the intended use and user(s) identified and accurate?		

In the format of a spreadsheet, the Universal Business Process Model Quality Criteria can be filtered by model component, quality factor, and level of assessment. The following information can be recorded about each criterion:

Criteria Met – The reviewer's opinion of whether or not the quality criteria have been met. It is a Yes or No answer.

Comment/Reason – When the quality criteria are not met and that assessment is No, this field contains the reviewer's comment or reason why not. The reviewer may recommend or propose the corrective action that should be taken to meet that Quality Criteria.

Exercise 6 – Validate Business Process Model

Review the notes provided to validate the model and recommend quality improvements.

Henry Woo, business analyst, CACHE project, drops by your desk with this process model.

"Here's a more detailed view of the Create/Update Bid process design that I put together this morning. What do you think?"

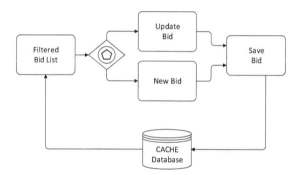

Validate the notation quality and offer review comments to improve its syntactical quality. Validate the key stakeholder participation quality and offer comments to improve its contextual quality.

Compare your results to the proposed solution at www.ProcessModelingAdvisor.com.

CONCLUSION

Establish, manage, and optimise your business process modeling competence by adopting the defined and proven Universal Process Modeling Procedure.

In 1989, Watts S. Humphrey raised awareness in North America about a process maturity framework and a methodology for managing the software process (*Managing the Software Process, Watts S. Humphrey, 1989, Addison-Wesley Publishing*). It defined five levels of maturity that characterise how a product is produced: Initial, repeatable, defined, measured, and managed. These maturity levels are today a widely recognized quality management concept. These five levels of maturity can be used to characterise your process modeling maturity or competence:

Level 1 – Initial – How you produce a business process model is ad-hoc. You invent or reinvent how to develop a business process model as you try to produce one by trial and error. The contextual and syntactical qualities of the resulting process model are predictably unreliable.

Level 2 – Repeatable – How you produce a business process model is repeatable, based on past experience. The syntactical and contextual qualities of the resulting business process model are contingent upon your own memory and experience, so it is predictably unique, perhaps incomplete, or archaic by today's standards.

Level 3 – Defined – How you produce a business process model has itself been defined as a procedure that you follow. Your process modeling skill or competence is demonstrated by following this defined process or procedure in the face of all the other dynamic stakeholders, constraints and opportunities surrounding this modeling work. The quality of the resulting business process model is predictably similar from one model to the next and for anyone else who follows the same procedure. In the face of unique project constraints and opportunities, you will stick with the procedure and produce a predictably high-quality process model.

Level 4 – Managed – The defined steps you take to produce a business process model is measured at some level and you can seek to improve it. You are at least are aware of key process model factors like the process model's development effort, review comments/defects you encounter, rework effort you need to spend, model size, and timeliness. This awareness enables you to better estimate and predict your effort and productivity and identify areas for improvement in your process modeling approach.

Level 5 – Optimized – A process model's production is improved in response to its measured performance. You are able to tune or optimise your process modeling approach based on your attention to past effort, review comments/defects, and rework effort and time spent. You decide to improve on or tailor your elicitation techniques, the time you spend, the types of key stakeholder participation, or modeling tools, based observed or anticipated key factors.

Why use the UPMP as your defined process for process modeling? It will improve your chances of producing high-quality business process models within BPM or IT projects. It will enable you, either a beginner or experienced business process modeler, to establish or define and improve your business process modeling competence. If you are a beginner, adopting the defined approach of the Universal Process Modeling Procedure will help you to quickly establish your process-modeling competence and provide you the benefits of a defined process. If you are an experienced process modeler then you can use the Universal Business Process Modeling Procedure to validate your existing approach, and begin to measure and improve areas of your process modeling competence. This will result in a business process model of predictably consistent quality in the face of unique project dynamics. If you can achieve these benefits, then you can spend more time doing other important tasks in BPM or IT projects.

APPENDIX 1 – THE UNIVERSAL BUSINESS PROCESS MODEL ELICITATION AGENDAS

Conduct elicitation activities (e.g. a workshop, an interview, etc.) using the Universal Business Process Model Elicitation Agendas.

A business analyst may use various elicitation techniques throughout a business process model's development.

For example, a business analyst may define and verify the model's mission by reviewing a project plan, and meeting with the project manager or team. A team might set out to develop a process' scope, and basic flow in a single workshop, with the intent of reconvening later in further workshops or interviews to elicit refinements and then validate the model. In any case, a business analyst needs a clear and concise agenda in each of these engagements.

A key to success while eliciting a model's content is to be asking the right questions. Select the agenda for a business process elicitation activity from the consolidated Universal Business Process Model Elicitation Agendas, depending on the model component whose content will be elicited. Each component agenda is focused on eliciting meaningful content for a business process model component: mission, scope, basic flow, activity definitions, process flow refinements, or validation.

Universal Business Process Model Mission Elicitation Agenda:

1) What is the intended use of this model and who will use it?
2) Will this model describe a business process in its current state or a future state?
3) What is this model's required degree of abstraction?

Universal Scope Elicitation Agenda:

1) What is the name of this process or function?
2) Who or what are the external actors that surround this process or function?
3) What does this process or function give to or get from each of its external actors?

Universal Basic Business Process Flow Elicitation Agenda:

1) What causes this process to start?
2) What happens next? (Once answered, the question is repeated.)
3) What is the expected outcome of this process?

Universal Business Activity Definition Elicitation Agenda:

1) What are the candidate business activities?
2) Does each candidate business activity pass the Universal Business Process Definition?
   - Is it a repeatable collection of related work tasks? What are they?
   - Is it initiated in response to a business event? What is it or are they?
   - Does it have an expected outcome? What is it or are they?
   - Who or what is its customer or customers?

Universal Business Process Flow Refinement Elicitation Agendas:

Activity Decomposition

1) What causes this activity to start?
2) What is the expected outcome of this activity?
3) What tasks need to be performed to achieve the expected outcome this activity?

Activity Summarization

1) What is the initiating event of the first activity in the sequence flow to be summarised?
2) What are the activities in the sequence flow to be summarised?
3) What is the expected outcome of the last activity in the sequence flow to be summarised?

Conditional Work

1) 1) Is what happens next in the business process flow unconditional? If not, what business rule dictates, or business decision needs to be made, about what happens next?
2) What is the conditional work activity?

Errors and Interruptions (aka Exceptions)

1) What could cause either an activity or the entire process not to reach its expected outcome during the execution of a) each activity, or b) the entire process?
2) What extra activity or work will need to be performed to resolve the exception?

Delays

1) Can each activity start as soon as its preceding activity in the business process flow finishes? If not, then when?

Data Input and Output

1) What inputs are received and outputs are produced by each activity in this business process?
2) What is the source and what is the target of each input and output?

Assigned Responsibilities

1) Who or what is responsible for performing (achieving the expected outcome of) each activity in the business process?

Related Datasets and Specifications

1) What process-related datasets or specifications are relevant to each activity or this entire business process?

Event-Oriented Business Process Flow

1) What outcome needs to be achieved before the start of each business activity in this business process?

APPENDIX 2 – UNIVERSAL PROCESS MODEL QUALITY CHECKLIST

Universal Process Model Fitness For Use Quality Checklist

1. Is this model good enough for its intended use?

> 1.1 Is this model's contextual quality good enough for its intended use?
>
>> 1.1.1 Is this model's business accuracy good enough for its intended use?
>>
>> *For more detailed criteria, refer to Universal Business Accuracy Quality Checklist.*
>>
>> 1.1.2 Is this model's key stakeholder participation quality good enough for its intended use?
>>
>> *For more detailed criteria, refer to Universal Key Stakeholder Participation Quality Checklist.*
>
> 1.2 Is this model's syntactical quality good enough for its intended use?
>
>> 1.2.1 Is this model's configuration quality good enough for its intended use?
>>
>> *For more detailed criteria, refer to Universal Model Configuration Quality Checklist.*
>>
>> 1.2.2 Is this model's notation quality good enough for its intended use?
>>
>> *For more detailed criteria, refer to Universal BPMN Notation Quality Checklist.*

Universal Business Accuracy Quality Checklist

1. Is the model's mission statement accurate?

    1.1 Is the model's required tense (current or future) defined and accurate?

    1.2 Is the model's required degree of abstraction (conceptual, logical, or configuration) defined and accurate?

    1.3 Are model's the intended use and user(s) identified and accurate?

2. Is the model's scope diagram accurate enough for the model's intended use?

    2.1 Is the scope diagram's process name accurate enough?

    2.2 Are the scope diagram's external actors accurate enough?

    2.3 Are the scope diagram's exchanges between the business process and its external actors accurate enough?

3. Is the model's basic business process flow diagram(s) accurate enough for the model's intended use?

    3.1 Is what causes the process to start (start event) accurate enough?

    3.2 Is the basic activity flow accurate enough?

    3.3 Is the expected outcome (or outcomes) (end event) accurate enough?

    2.4 Is the model's Activity Catalogue accurate enough?

    3.5 Are the Activity Catalogue's activity definitions accurate enough?

  5. Are the process flow diagram refinements accurate enough?

    Decomposition or summary of business activities?

Business Decision Logic?

Exceptions and Delays?

Assigned Responsibilities?

Universal Key Stakeholder Participation Quality Checklist

1. Was the Mission of this business process model elicited and reviewed with key stakeholders?

Who participated in the mission's elicitation?

Who participated in the model's review?

2. Was the Scope of this business process model elicited and reviewed with key stakeholders?

Who participated in the scope diagram's elicitation?

Who participated in the scope diagram's review?

3. Was the Activity Catalogue of this business process model elicited and reviewed with key stakeholders?

Who participated in the Activity Catalogue's elicitation?

Who participated in the Activity Catalogue's review?

4. Was the Basic Business Process Flow(s) of this business process model elicited and reviewed with key stakeholders?

Who participated in the basic business process flow's elicitation?

Who participated in the basic business process flow's review?

5. Was the Refined Business Process Flow(s) of this business process model elicited and reviewed with key stakeholders?

Who participated in the refined business process flow's elicitation?

Who participated in the refined business process flow's review?

Universal Model Configuration Quality Checklist

1. Does the business process model include a mission statement?

> 1.1 Does the mission statement include the essential process modeling mission parameters: 1) tense, 2) degree of abstraction, and 3) intended use/user?

2. Does the business process model include a scope diagram?

> 2.1 Does the scope model include the three essential scope diagram elements: 1) named boundary, 2) external actors and 3) exchanges?

3. Does the business process model include an Activity Catalogue?

> 3.1 Does each activity in the business process model appear in the Activity Catalogue?

> 3.2 Does each activity in the Activity Catalogue have a definition?

4. Does the business model include at least a basic process flow diagram?

> 4.1 Does the business process flow diagram include the basic business process flow diagram elements: 1) initiating event, 2) succession of activities and 3) expected outcome (end event)?

5. Does the business process flow diagram(s) include the types of refinements needed to meet the model's intended use?

> *Decomposed Business Activities? Summarized Business Activities? Decision Logic? Data Inputs and Outputs? Exceptions? Delays? Assigned Responsibilities? Related Process Datasets and Specifications? External Stakeholder Interactions? Event-*

Oriented Flow?

Universal BPMN Notation Quality Checklist

1. Is the mission statement written in plain language?

2. Does the scope diagram use BPMN notation well enough?

2.1 Does the scope diagram use BPMN Pools as expected?

2.2 Does the scope diagram use BPMN Message Flows as expected?

2.3 Do the BPMN Pools and Message Flows have text labels as expected?

3. Does the basic business process flow diagram use BPMN notation well enough?

3.1 Is the initiating event illustrated using the best-suited BPMN Start Event flow object?

3.2 Is each activity illustrated using the best-suited BPMN Task or Sub-Process flow object?

3.3 Is the expected outcome illustrated using the best-suited BPMN End Event flow object?

4. Is the Activity Catalogue written in plain language?

4.1 Is each activity named using a Verb-Subject pattern?

5. Do the business process flow diagram refinements use BPMN well enough?

5.1 Is each activity illustrated using a BPMN Task or BPMN Sub-Process?

5.2 Is every business decision illustrated using the best-suited BPMN OR Gateway object?

5.3 Is every parallel split in flow illustrated using a BPMN AND Gateway object?

5.4 Is every convergence of parallel split flow illustrated using a BPMN Join Gateway object?

5.5 Is every business process exception or delay illustrated using the best-suited BPMN Intermediate Event object?

5.6 Does every BPMN Message Flow use a dashed line (not a solid line)?

5.7 Is each external actor illustrated as a BPMN Pool?

5.8 Is each assigned role illustrated as a BPMN Lane?

5.9 (Activity Decomposition) Does the business process flow diagram illustrate business activities using the accepted modeling notation? If so:

> 5.9.1 Is every activity that is decomposed elsewhere in the model illustrated using a BPMN sub-process?

> 5.9.2 Is every activity that is not decomposed elsewhere in the model illustrated using a BPMN task?

5.10 (Business Decision Logic) Does the business process flow diagram illustrate Decision Logic using the accepted modeling notation?

> 5.10.1 Is each business decision illustrated using the best-suited BPMN gateway?

> 5.10.2 Is each gateway annotated with brief text describing the decision and conditions?

5.11 (External Actor Interactions) Does the business process flow diagram illustrate external actor Interaction details using the accepted modeling notation?

> 5.11.1 Is each exchange between a business activity or event and any external actor illustrated using a BPMN message flow?

> 5.11.2 Is each exchange labelled to describe what is exchanged?

5.12 (Interruptions, Delays and Errors) Does the business process flow diagram illustrate process interruptions, delays, or errors using the accepted modeling notation?

> 5.12.1 Is every interruption, delay, or error illustrated using the best-suited BPMN intermediate event object?

5.13 (Assigned Responsibilities) Does the process flow diagram illustrate assigned responsibilities using the accepted modeling notation?

> 5.13.1 Is the business process illustrated using a BPMN pool?

> 5.13.2 Is every role illustrated using a BPMN lane?

> 5.13.3 Is every activity in the business process flow allocated to one lane or another?

5.14 (Event-Oriented Business Process Flow) Does the business process flow diagram illustrate event-oriented business flow using the accepted modeling notation?

> 5.14.1 Is each initiating event illustrated using the best-suited BPMN Start Event object?

> 5.14.2 Is each activity illustrated using the best-suited BPMN Task or Sub-process flow object?

> 5.14.3 Is each expected outcome illustrated using the

best-suited BPMN End Event object?

5.14.4 Are start and end events labelled to indicate the named initiating event or expected outcome?

5.15 (Process-Related Data and Documentation) Does the business process flow diagram illustrate process-related data and/or documentation using the accepted modeling notation?

5.15.1 Is each associated data object or document illustrated using the appropriate BPMN data object or data store icon?

5.15.2 Is each association labelled using a BPMN association (not a sequence flow or message flow)?

Appendix 3 - Using BPMN Start Event and End Event Sub-Types

How to Illustrate Business Process Initiation Using BPMN Start Event Sub-Types

Use the best-suited BPMN start event flow object to illustrate what causes a business process to start.

BPMN offers a set of start event objects to choose from. Each is intended to graphically communicate what type of start event initiates the process.

The BPMN start event flow objects are:

	Start	
None	◯	Generic/Unspecified or start of called sub-process
Mail	✉	A message arrives from another process or external actor.
Timer	🕐	A specific date/time or time limit/schedule is reached.
Rule	目	A condition, defined by a business rule, becomes true.
Multiple	⬠	Any one of a set of conditions has occurred.

The model's mission, specifically the model's required degree of abstraction and intended use, should guide the BPMN start event flow object chosen to illustrate a process start event.

If the model's mission is to produce a process' conceptual degree of abstraction to a business audience, then a BPMN None (generic) start event flow object is probably the best choice. It can conceptually communicate what (now how) the initiating event is, which is what is of interest to a conceptual model's reader, without also communicating the logical start event subtype, which is not.

If the model's mission is to produce a logical degree of abstraction of a process to a business audience (e.g. a value stream map within a BPM project), then a BPMN start event flow object sub-type (e.g. message, timer, rule, multiple) may be of interest to that model's audience.

If the model's mission is to produce a logical or configuration model that will be used by a software programmer, then a more specific BPMN start event flow object may be of interest to that model's software programming audience.

Examples of the BPMN None, Message, Timer, Rule, and Multiple flow objects' uses are described further in the remaining subsections of this chapter.

USING A BPMN GENERIC (NONE) START EVENT
If the model's degree of abstraction is conceptual or the event type is inconsequential to the model's intended use or reader, then illustrate the process' start using a BPMN None start event.

The BPMN None start event object might be better named "Generic" because every business process is initiated in response to something. Use the BPMN None start event flow object in a conceptual process model or logical process model when the type of event that causes a process to start when is undetermined, or at the start of a called process (subroutine).

Conceptual Model – If the mission is to produce a conceptual model, then use the BPMN None start event flow object to illustrate the process' start event. Using the other start event types may just confuse the reader and are unnecessary to meet the mission of a conceptual model.

Undetermined – If the type of event that causes the business process to begin is not yet clear, or no other BPMN start event flow object is better suited to illustrate the event, then use the BPMN None object. For example, when first developing the model, the arrival of a passenger at an airline counter or kiosk to start the Airport Check-in business process may be best illustrated as a BPMN None object instead of a BPMN

Message, Timer, Rule, or Multiple start event flow object. The start event type of a logical or configuration model can be changed when the process model is refined in UPMP Step 5.

Called Sub-process– If the process is initiated by being called as a sub-process, then use the BPMN None object. In this procedural software-programming context, the calling process controls when the sub-process is performed by calling it as a subroutine.

NOTATION
The BPMN None Start event notation is a circle, not in bold, with an empty center.

EXAMPLE
We may have observed that the Airport Check-in business process starts when a passenger arrives for check-in (at check-in counter or kiosk). This event is not a message, timer, rule, or multiple start event, so the BPMN None object is the best option.

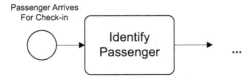

USING A BPMN MESSAGE START EVENT
If receiving a request or message starts the process, then illustrate its start using a BPMN Message start event.

Use the BPMN Message start event object (in a logical or configuration process model) to illustrate that a business process is caused to start by the arrival of a request or input (electronic, verbal information, or material) received from another process, system, organization, or person.

NOTATION
The BPMN Message start event notation is: a circle, not in bold, with an

"envelope" in the center.

EXAMPLE

The Check No-Fly List business process starts whenever a No-Fly List Inquiry arrives from any authorized system in the airport security network.

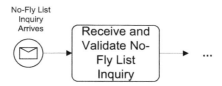

USING A BPMN TIMER START EVENT

If the process is started by a schedule or time interval then illustrate its start using a BPMN Timer start event.

Use the BPMN Timer start event flow object (in a logical or configuration process model) to illustrate that a business process is caused to start by a schedule, time interval, or point in time.

NOTATION

The BPMN Timer start event notation is a circle, not in bold, with a "clock" in the center.

EXAMPLE

Thirty minutes before a scheduled flight is scheduled to board, the Board Flight process begins.

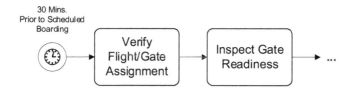

A business process might be caused to start after a certain time interval instead of at a pre-determined point in time. The passing of that time interval is an event. It is also modeled as a BPMN timer start event. For example, at the end of every 90-minute interval, a Security Walkthrough process is started.

USING A BPMN RULE START EVENT

Use a BPMN Rule start event flow object to illustrate that a process is started by a logical condition, defined by a policy or rule, becoming true.

Use the BPMN Rule start event flow object (in a logical or configuration process model) to illustrate that the business process is caused to start by a condition defined by a business rule or policy. The business rule or policy defined is a state that when true causes the process to begin.

NOTATION

The BPMN rule start event notation is a circle, not in bold, with a "list" in the center.

EXAMPLE

It is a regulation (business policy or rule) that a passenger must accompany his or her checked baggage on an airline flight. If a passenger's checked baggage is on the plane by the time the gate is closed, but the passenger is not, then the (Deplane) Pull Baggage process will start.

Checked baggage is on board, but the checked-in passenger is not and the gate has been closed, so the Pull Baggage process begins.

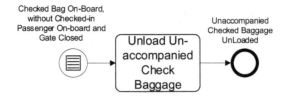

USING A BPMN MULTIPLE START EVENT

If any one of several possible business conditions can start the process, then use a BPMN Multiple start event to illustrate its start.

Use a BPMN Multiple start event flow object (in a logical or configuration process model) to illustrate a business process that is started by <u>any one</u> of a set of possible events. When any one of the sets of events occurs, the business process will start.

NOTATION

The BPMN multiple start event notation is a circle, not in bold, with a "star" in the center.

EXAMPLE

The Update Airport Arrival/Departure Schedule process will begin whenever any one of the following events occurs:

- A flight is delayed or expedited (by another airport or in-flight).
- A flight lands.
- A gate is reassigned.
- A flight takes off.
- A flight is canceled.

How to Illustrate a Business Process' Expected Outcome using BPMN End Event Sub-Types

Illustrate a business process' expected outcome(s) using the best-suited BPMN end event flow object.

A business process' expected outcome is one of its defining elements, so a process' expected outcome should always be included in its business process flow diagram.

BPMN offers different end event objects that may be used to illustrate expected outcomes. Once the expected outcome has been elicited, an object must be chosen from among the available BPMN end event objects to illustrate the end of any process' basic business process flow.

Which BPMN end event object illustrates a process' end depends on the model's mission, specifically its required degree of abstraction and intended use. According to the UPMP, every model has a required degree of abstraction and intended use. (These are defined by the model's mission in UPMP Step 1.)

If the model's intended use is to describe workflow to a business audience (such as a value stream map within a BPM project) then a conceptual or logical degree of abstraction is likely required of the model. Using the BPMN None (Generic) end event object makes practical sense. If the business analyst is not certain which BPMN end event object to use, he or she should use this one.

If the model's intended use requires a physical/configuration degree of abstraction for the model, then using a more specific end event object makes sense as long as it will be meaningful to the model's intended audience.

Practical examples of BPMN end event object uses, including None (Generic), Message, and Multiple are described further in the following subsections. There are other BPMN end events. We will not demonstrate them here, as their practical uses are limited to software-programming logic.

End

None	○	Generic/Unspecified or end of called sub-process
Message	◉	Message has been sent
Multiple	◉	Multiple outcomes

BPMN None (Generic) End Event – If the model's mission calls for a conceptual degree of abstraction, then use a BPMN None (hereafter referred to as Generic) end event to illustrate the end event of the process.

If the model's mission calls for a logical or configuration degree of abstraction, then consider using the specific BPMN End event objects:

BPMN Message End Event – used to illustrate where a business process has reached its expected outcome with a message transmitted or sent to another process, system, organization, or person.

BPMN Multiple End Event – used to illustrate where a business process has reached its expected outcome, which consists of multiple expected outcomes that are contained in a single graphical event.

Other types of BPMN end event objects exist. They are typically useful to illustrate alternate outcomes, such as when a process ends earlier than expected, in a refined business process flow. These end event flow objects are demonstrated in UPMP Step 5 – Refine Business Process Flow(s).

Each model's unique mission should dictate which end event object to use to illustrate the expected outcome of any business process flow diagram. The following subsections describe how BPMN end event objects can typically be used to illustrate a business process' expected outcome.

USING BPMN NONE (GENERIC END EVENT

If the model's degree of abstraction is conceptual or the event type is inconsequential to the model's intended use or reader, then illustrate the outcome using the BPMN None end event.

)Note: The term "generic" is perhaps a better name for the BPMN None end event object. The term "None" also literally means that there is no expected outcome, contradicting a key tenant of the Universal Business Process Definition: Every business process has an expected outcome.

The BPMN standard intends the None end event flow object to illustrate the end of a called software sub-process (or subroutine), which is meaningful in a software programming context. However, business analysts and process analysts can use the BPMN None end event object in other practical ways for business process modeling, to illustrate the expected outcome of a business process flow.

There are at least a couple of practical uses for the BPMN None end event flow object.

The expected outcome of a business process flow is reached, but at the time a model is first drawn, the business analyst may not yet have elicited enough information to decide which type of end event is best suited to illustrate the end event. The analyst may come back later to refine the event subtype and the BPMN icon.

If the model's required degree of abstraction is conceptual, then then the end event will be best illustrated as a None end event. Illustrating the end event type generically keeps the conceptual model simple, and best suits its mission for its intended reader.

NOTATION
The BPMN None end event notation is a circle, bolded, with an empty center.

EXAMPLE
In this example, a BPMN generic end event is used to illustrate where the Check Baggage sub-process comes to an end. The Attach Baggage Tags activity is the last activity in the basic flow of the Check Baggage sub-process of the Airline Check-in business process. *The expected outcome of the Check Baggage sub-process is that the baggage has been checked. The Check Baggage sub-process activity is elaborated on in its own diagram. Its last activity is Attach Baggage Tags.* When the Attach Baggage Tags activity has been completed, the Check Baggage sub-process reaches its expected outcome (Baggage Checked) and the Check Baggage sub-process has reached its expected outcome.

USING THE BPMN MESSAGE END EVENT

If the process' expected outcome is something sent to another process, person, organization, or system, then illustrate the outcome using the BPMN Message end event.

The BPMN Message end event may be used to illustrate that the expected outcome of a business process is reached when an output has been sent to another process, system, or person. (In certain software process models, it may be necessary to show that process outputs are sent and received as electronic messages. BPMN Message end events may, in turn, be graphically connected to BPMN Message flows.)

For example, the last activity of an invoicing process may be to submit the invoice. The outcome of the flow is that an invoice has been sent, which makes the BPMN Message end event type best suited to illustrate this end event.

NOTATION
The BPMN Message end event notation is a circle, bolded, with an "envelope" in the center.

EXAMPLE
When the Broadcast Flight Delay activity is completed, the Notify of Flight Delay business process has achieved its expected outcome. A BPMN Message end event is used to illustrate where the Notify of Flight Delay business process flow ends. The BPMN Message end event illustrates that a flight delay notification has been sent, which is the end of the Broadcast Flight Delay Notification business process.

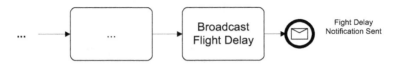

USING BPMN MULTIPLE END EVENT

If the process has multiple expected outcomes, then illustrate the outcomes using the BPMN Multiple end event.

The BPMN Multiple end event can be used to illustrate that a business process will end when <u>all</u> of a set of expected outcomes has occurred. All of the outcomes in the set are illustrated using a single BPMN Multiple end event in the business process flow diagram.

For example, there are multiple, inclusive expected outcomes of the Airport Check-in process. They are: 1) that the passenger has been issued a boarding pass, and 2) that the passenger's bags have been checked. The BPMN Multiple end event type is best suited to illustrate these multiple outcomes as a single process-ending event.

NOTATION
The BPMN Multiple end event notation is a circle, bolded, with a pentagon in the center.

EXAMPLE
The Airport Check-in business process has two expected outcomes: 1) that the passenger has been issued a boarding pass, and 2) that baggage has been checked.

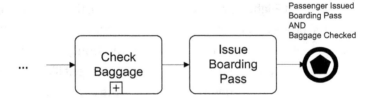

ABOUT THE AUTHOR

Edmund Metera is a senior project manager whose more than three decades of business system and process consulting experience spans a broad spectrum of industries and project profiles. Ed teaches IIBA-registered courses and serves as an advisor to the Northern Alberta Institute of Technology's Corporate and Computer Training Center's Business Analysis Certificate Program. He has taught and mentored business analysts, process analysts, and managers for professional organizations such as IIBA and PMI.

INDEX

model configuration, 183; modeling
notation, 184; review techniques,
185

R

Refinements: choosing, 107; common
types, 105
Related Datasets and Specifications:
defined, 159; elicitation, 160;
example, 161, 164; illustrate, 163
Rule-based Work: definition, 117

S

Scope: boundary, 59; definition, 59;
elicitation, 59; example, 64, 68;

external actors, 62
Six Sigma, 9

T

Total Quality Management, 9

U

Universal Business Process Definition:
benefits, 37; defined, 38; rationale,
36
Universal Process Modeling Procedure
(UPMP): overview, 21–29
UPMP: capability maturity, 191;
defined process, 192; products, 30

www.ingramcontent.com/pod-product-compliance
Lightning Source LLC
Chambersburg PA
CBHW071114050326
40690CB00008B/1221